"It is with great pleasure that I highly recommend *Spiritual Care for People Living with Dementia Using Multisensory Interventions*. Dr. Behers has done a tremendous amount of research in preparing this book. I have been honored to be able to assist him by photographing the needed pictures. With sight, combined with the other senses, many have come and will come to an awakening in this life."

—*Carol A. Gilmore, MMin*

"Richard Behers shows us the true path to communicating with these special patients. While many people continue to try to 'reach' them with verbal communication, Behers knows that the best—and often only—way is through the senses."

—*Marian Betancourt, author and journalist,*
former senior writer, HealthCare Chaplaincy Network

of related interest

Facilitating Spiritual Reminiscence for People with Dementia
A Learning Guide
Elizabeth MacKinlay and Corinne Trevitt
ISBN 978 1 84905 573 4
eISBN 978 1 78450 018 4

Sensory Modulation in Dementia Care
Assessment and Activities for Sensory-Enriched Care
Tina Champagne
ISBN 978 1 78592 733 1
eISBN 978 1 78450 427 4

Spiritual Care in Allied Health Practice
Edited by Lindsay B. Carey, PhD and Bernice A. Mathisen, PhD
Foreword by Harold Koenig
ISBN 978 1 78592 220 6
eISBN 978 1 78450 501 1

Spirituality in Hospice Care
How Staff and Volunteers Can Support the Dying and Their Families
Edited by Andrew Goodhead and Nigel Hartley
Foreword by the Rt Revd Dr Barry Morgan
ISBN 978 1 78592 102 5
eISBN 978 1 78450 368 0

Spiritual Care in Common Terms
How Chaplains Can Effectively Describe the Spiritual
Needs of Patients in Medical Records
Gordon J. Hilsman, DMin
Foreword by James H. Gunn
ISBN 978 1 78592 724 9
eISBN 978 1 78450 369 7

Critical Care
Delivering Spiritual Care in Healthcare Contexts
Edited by Jonathan Pye, Peter Sedgwick and Andrew Todd
ISBN 978 1 84905 497 3
eISBN 978 0 85700 901 2

Spiritual Care for People Living with Dementia Using Multisensory Interventions

A Practical Guide for Chaplains

RICHARD BEHERS

Afterword by Carol Gilmore

Jessica Kingsley *Publishers*
London and Philadelphia

The accompanying photographs and video files can be downloaded
from www.jkp.com/voucher using the code TUYNETE

First published in 2018
by Jessica Kingsley Publishers
73 Collier Street
London N1 9BE, UK
and
400 Market Street, Suite 400
Philadelphia, PA 19106, USA

www.jkp.com

Copyright © Richard Behers 2018
Afterword copyright © Carol Gilmore 2018

Library of Congress Cataloging in Publication Data
A CIP catalog record for this book is available from the Library of Congress

British Library Cataloguing in Publication Data
A CIP catalogue record for this book is available from the British Library

ISBN 978 1 78592 811 6
eISBN 978 1 78450 856 2

Printed and bound in Great Britain

It is with the deepest humility and gratitude that I dedicate this work to my wife, Connie, for her support. In addition, I include Carol Gilmore, the photographer who captured the "one thing only" in each photograph that accompanies this book as part of the downloadable material. Also, I thank my hospice colleagues for their encouragement to stay the course with the Dementia Care Protocol.

Contents

Preface

"I don't know what I am doing." That is not such an inspiring statement to make your first day on the job. But that was how I felt. I went from one resident room to another and met with men and women with dementia. There was no preparation for what I faced. What a nightmare!

Oh, I learned the medical facts about Alzheimer's disease and other dementias, but no one educated me how to communicate with those living with this condition. After visiting with each resident and attempting to provide spiritual support, I went to the office feeling like a failure. I called a few friends who were veteran hospice chaplains and asked them what they did to provide ministry to those they served who lived with dementia. The common theme among these veteran chaplains was music. That was the sum total of what they provided.

I knew I could sing, so I went to see this group of people living with dementia. I sang "Amazing Grace," "Jesus Loves Me," "It is Well with My Soul," and it was amazing! Some actually looked at me. Others mouthed words to the hymns, and one other sang a few words. That inspired me.

Then I thought that there had to be something more I could do to enhance their spiritual care. Several years later, I put together what we call the Dementia Care Protocol which features a multisensory intervention.

My assumption is that you are a chaplain or spiritual caregiver. It is my desire and prayer that the words on the pages will inspire you to integrate what you read into your ministry. I can't wait to hear your stories!

Introduction

God remembers his child who has dementia when they can't remember Him. They are not alone.[1]

The dilemma

My first day on the job as a hospice chaplain unfolded in a way I would never have imagined. I arrived at the long-term care facility prepared to provide spiritual support to those persons on my caseload. I noticed they all had Alzheimer's disease or another form of dementia. Actually, I thought I was prepared for what was ahead of me.

The facility staff member directed me to the residents' rooms. I arrived at the first room and knocked on the door. There was no response. I knocked again, still no response. A facility staff member came by and recognized my predicament and instructed, "Just go in. None of the patients can talk, so don't worry about manners, just go in." So I did.

Mrs. Jones[2] was lying on her bed, her arms stretched out reaching for that which was not there. I walked over to her bed and introduced myself to her. There was no cognition

---

1 Author's own words.
2 All names are pseudonyms.

that I was present. I said my name once more. Again, she did not respond. Not knowing what to do, I did what any chaplain would do and said a prayer and left. This experience was repeated throughout my visits that day. It was enough to cause me to question my calling into hospice chaplaincy. I pondered my plight of ignorance of any methodology to connect with these persons. It was clear to me in my work with non-dementia patients that chaplaincy had a lot to do with building relationships with patients so that trust was built. Building trust with someone living with dementia would be a new experience for me and one that would change the way I practiced chaplaincy.

A family caregiver of one of the patients living with dementia opened her arms to me when she observed how I worked with her loved one. Conversations of deep existential and spiritual issues ensued. I listened intently to her journey through the morass which is dementia. Good days, bad days, really bad days typified her experience.

As I got to know other caregivers, I noticed a theme arose in nearly every discussion. They would tear up when it came to touching on the subject of a nursing facility and feeling they had no other choice but to place their loved one in a long-term care facility. I am convinced family caregivers will receive a reward for their incredible acts of love and servanthood. Yes, I understand when I hear their guilt and shame for losing their patience with their loved one. However, I am moved when I hear of their Herculean efforts to feed, bathe, change adult diapers, clean their loved one up after a particularly messy bowel movement, and/or ensure their loved one is safe by literally barricading the doors with multiple locks so their loved one does not run away. I have an idea that this massive host of family caregivers will receive diamonds in their heavenly crowns. They earned them. I am indebted to them as many became my teachers. They lived out before me virtues of fidelity, loyalty, tenacity, and love without limits. They taught me that there is no quitting time. They keep on regardless.

What is a chaplain to do?

How was I prepared to do this work of providing spiritual care to patients with dementia in the end stage? Simply put, I wasn't prepared. I went through the three-hour Alzheimer's course, and I even had another hour of classroom work on the disease. The fact is that background information, while important, did not prepare me for my ministry to these patients. That is why I constructed this book as I have. Before we can learn how to engage the patient with the multisensory intervention, we need to know something about the condition. To go blindly into a patient's room or facility with no knowledge of the disease process is foolish. Further, when the chaplain attends an interdisciplinary team meeting and the medical terms are being bandied about, it would be a good idea for the chaplain to know what those terms mean. So, indeed, the three or four hours of education I received enabled me to understand the medical part of the disease. I suppose the agency figured that the chaplains would figure out the spiritual part themselves. So I did. And that makes up the balance of the book. It is my commitment to you, the reader, to give you all I have accumulated through the years so you can implement the multisensory intervention in your own ministry. You can download the key components of this multisensory intervention at www.jkp.com/voucher using the code TUYNETE. I urge you to excel in your ministry to patients with dementia, because there are so many living with this condition. I appeal to pastors, priests, imams, rabbis, and other spiritual care leaders to learn how to minister to those in your congregation who cannot attend because of their dementia, but are in desperate need of your presence. You have what they need. Likewise, I urge hospice and hospital chaplains to excel in this intervention as your patients and their families will rise up and call you blessed for your labor of love. To be sure, this is a work that will cost you time and effort, not to mention the skills you will develop as you prepare and engage in this intervention.

Figuring out how to connect

After my first day attempting to minister to my patients, I went home and contacted several chaplain friends of mine. "What do you do with patients with dementia?" Their answers did not provide much insight, but I did hear a common theme—music. These chaplains used boom boxes, a dated term to describe a large compact disc player with rather large speakers. I didn't have one of those, so I planned to just use my own voice. With that new tool, I went back to see if music could help. It did!

Finally, a breakthrough of sorts! From music I ventured forward to trial and error with pictures taken from magazines that might interest the patient. It was soon evident that the patients could not see what I had hoped they would. Their condition was too far advanced for them to pick out a flower from a photograph display of beautiful flowers and fruits.

Researching the provision of care for people living with dementia was next on my list of actions to take. I read Eileen Shamy's book *A Guide to the Spiritual Dimension of Care for People with Alzheimer's Disease and Related Dementia* (2003). The subtitle to her book crystalizes my perspective on persons living with dementia: *More than Body, Brain and Breath*. In a conversation with another chaplain recently we discussed how society views persons who are no longer productive with their lives. The most vulnerable of these persons is the dementia population. It seems that in some long-term care facilities these are the persons that get just enough care to keep them alive. Larry Gardiner (2012), who himself lives with dementia, said:

The ego leaves quite early. I become what I have always been. It allows me to become quite naughty. I am unstoppable and unbiddable. But they park people like me in a warehouse with other people like me, and it diminishes me. I believe more people die of depression and despair than of dementia.

I agree with Mr. Gardiner. From my experience visiting some nursing facilities, there are so few activities for residents living with dementia that they just sit in their wheelchairs or lie in bed with no mental, emotional, or physical stimulation. This is why the multisensory intervention is so effective. The process awakens the mind and the soul.

You can learn how to connect

Who will benefit from reading and implementing this approach to communicating with persons living with severe dementia? Chaplains, pastors, priests, imams, rabbis, and other spiritual leaders can and will gain insight and confidence in providing spiritual support to these patients. In Chapter 2 of the book, I present characteristics of the most common forms of dementia combining medical terms and their application to pastoral care. In reflection upon my orientation experience in hospice, the medical terminology was the only thing taught. If a new employee was not a nurse or other medical type, you would find yourself lost in the new language. It took me well over six months to begin to understand the terminology. I recall a presentation made by a nurse regarding one of the dementia patients I was serving. She described the patient as cachectic. I thought I was missing something as I racked my brain to try to figure out what this condition was. At a break in the meeting, I rather sheepishly asked the nurse the meaning of the term. As I recall, she smiled and said something like this: "Rich, this is a medical term for severe loss of weight. It might be good for you to take notes on the new words, so you can understand these conversations in our interdisciplinary meetings." Ouch! I did take her advice and began taking notes on terms that I did not know. Before long, I was conversant in the new language. To make an analogy from the religious world, each denomination or world religion has its own language. If a nurse or physician came to a meeting among your colleagues and you used your specific religious jargon, I am sure they would be lost as well. It boils down to this: you, as a spiritual leader, need to be willing to learn a new language. This book will give guidance, definitions, and applications on what that new language describes. Your congregants are in need of your pastoral presence and care during this very difficult and vulnerable period of their lives. Having trained chaplains in this process and seeing them succeed in providing wonderfully compassionate and effective pastoral care, I can promise you this is a challenge you will find exceptionally rewarding. Your stature in the congregation will rise among the faithful. They will know their leader not only says s/he cares but actually reaches out to the most vulnerable among them.

Dr. John Zeisel wrote a masterful book on the topic of dementia care titled *I'm Still Here* (2009). For now, please note the title. While you may look at the patient, your congregant, or the person on your pastoral care caseload, as non-responsive and seemingly unreachable, note the title: "I'm Still Here." My impetus to develop a process to reach this large segment of my pastoral care caseload was this: "If you are still there, it is up to me to find you." I went on that mission and time and again I did find these wonderful persons and provided moments of peace and comfort they needed. Michael Verde, President of Memory Bridge, says:

> The next time you communicate with someone who is not at his or her cognitive best, remind yourself of this: "This interaction is not about me. This interaction is about someone who is seeking connection on terms that may not advance the interests or needs of my ego. I am going to go where your

needs are taking you. I am going to be with you in that place, wherever and however it is. I am going to let my ego disappear now. I am going to love you in your image instead of trying to re-create you in mine." (quoted in Greenblat 2012, p.88)

What Verde states so clearly is that we, as spiritual care practitioners, must check our egos in at the door and enter into the world of someone living with dementia. The content of this book will give you the skills to do just that. You are beginning a journey that will expand your ministry and bring you unspeakable inner joy, knowing you made a difference in a life others deemed unreachable.

Someone might ask, "Why a book on people at the end stage of dementia? After all, these people can't comprehend, talk, or in any other way communicate. Isn't this a waste of a spiritual caregiver's time?" I have heard this comment made on several occasions. It smacks of arrogance and ignorance. In a webinar I presented hosted by a major cognate group, I asked what I assumed would be a rather innocuous question: "Does your hospice allow you to have an ongoing spiritual support relationship with patients with dementia?" I was shocked when several indicated that they could not provide spiritual support to these patients. The rationale was that people living with a dementia would be a drag on the chaplain's time. At this juncture I will share the passion that inspires my ministry in hospice.

As I began my research into dementia care, I also discovered I knew little to nothing about the founding of the hospice movement. It didn't take long before I was introduced to the founder of the modern hospice movement, Dame Cicely Saunders. Her intrepid spirit drew me to the mission of caring for the dying. The term "movement" is a word chosen deliberately as the hospice has become more of an industry in 2017 than a movement. "Movement," however, captures the passion and ethos of what it means to be on the frontline in ministry to the patient and their families. The back story of the founding of the hospice by Dame Cicely Saunders highlights her intrepid, tenacious, and determined nature. The era in which she lived was that of World War II. Women were not encouraged to seek degrees other than teaching. Yet Dame Cicely was determined to become a nurse. Due to a back injury, she put her nursing career on hold and completed studies to become a medical social worker. As her career in the medical field developed, she made an astute observation that persons at the end of life not only could be treated better than they were, but must be treated better than they were. Because physicians would not listen to her new idea of how to care for the dying, she completed medical school as a full-fledged physician. Now, that is spirit! I see this type of indefatigable spirit every day in my work at the hospice. Spirit communicates with patients. They can sense when a physician or nurse or social worker or chaplain or CNA (certified nursing assistant) or volunteer has the right spirit. As long as I can, I will promote a hospice movement philosophy over the cold, calculating business model of a hospice industry.

While in medical school, Dame Cicely Saunders set herself apart from other medical students because of her love for patients. Was it due to the fact that she was an older student and, therefore, more mature? Or was it because she had a deep passion for people burning down deep in her soul? I'm not sure, I'll allow the reader to judge. I just know that her pattern was to read to the blind when she was on a break from formal training and take shifts as a caregiver to the dying.

In addition to the many legacy matters she left to the hospice movement, Saunders imparted a powerful quotation that is printed like a billboard for any hospice and a multifaceted philosophy of pain: "You matter because you are you, and you matter to the end of your life. We will do all we can not only to help you die peacefully but also to live until you die." There is something energizing about this statement. The spiritual caregiver is immediately drawn to it because that is the message of faith. "Live until you die" takes on a new meaning when providing care to patients with an end-stage dementia. These persons are unable to smile or carry on a conversation. Some are physically contracted by the virulence of the condition. Others project anger and violence if approached. Yet others are gentle and quite simply existing in the loneliness of a long-term care facility.

Saunders' social work background assisted her as she developed her philosophy of total pain. She observed that patients experienced social pain, spiritual pain, physical pain, and psychological pain. Chaplains have the privilege to plumb the depths of a patient's spiritual pain. In addition to that, chaplains may also explore with a patient his/her social pain and psychological pain. Of course, the chaplain will benefit from a broad education that would include pastoral care and counseling to enable him/her to be an effective source of inner comfort. The chaplain will also advocate for the patient in regard to physical pain. For example, a patient of mine was in the hospital. I paid him a visit and noticed signs of physical pain (wincing, and moving about from side to side in the bed). When I asked about his pain medication regimen, he mentioned that his next dose would not be for another hour. Because experience taught me that he probably had a PRN (*pro re nata*; as required) dose available, I excused myself from the room and went to the nurse's station to enquire. I respectfully spoke to the nurse indicating that this patient needed his dose of pain medication. She looked at his chart and stated his next dose would in an hour. I gently asked if she could check the chart for a PRN dose. She did and stated in amazement that he, indeed, had a note for PRN medication. She excused herself to get the medication and take it to the patient. Saunders did the medical community a tremendous service by laying the foundation for pain management.

Helping them live until they die

Live until you die looks like this: the patient was an 86-year-old woman with a diagnosis of dementia at the beginning of the late stage of dementia. When I first met her, she was in her wheelchair looking out of the large window that graced the common area of the small facility. As I approached her, I called her name. She then turned to me, and I observed that her eyes were swollen from crying. She looked at me and said, "My Mommy and Daddy are dead, and I am so sad." Her parents died years ago. I provided her comfort and told her how sorry I was that they had died. She needed the soothing words and touch of someone who cared. I provided care for her until she was 90 years of age. It was at this time that she no longer could speak but only was able to utter "Yes" or "No" after working hard to form the words. It was at this time that I had developed the multisensory intervention and was using it to provide care and hope for what I call "awakenings." Annie (not her real name) was seated in her high-back wheelchair in the common area of the facility. I then presented the multisensory intervention to her, and she had an awakening that was simply amazing. She began to speak to me in a conversational manner that made perfect sense for nearly five minutes. Facility personnel came out of other residents' rooms and the kitchen and watched what was happening with looks of disbelief on their faces. Annie's awakening ended when she saw someone who evoked fear within her. She said, "Trouble, trouble." The awakening ended, but it was amazing. The workers and facility owner asked me what I had done to cause such a wonderful experience. I told them that I believed I had developed a means to provide care for patients like Annie. I used it. It worked. Amazing! I served this patient until she died.

The motivation that drives my efforts

Most ministers and spiritual caregivers have not had formal training in providing spiritual care to those living at the end stage of dementia. It is assumed that the local parish minister will have contact with the patient and family who are members or affiliates of their faith center. That being the case, training in providing spiritual support is vital to a healthy pastoral care relationship. Gone are the days when the minister can simply rely on his suave and persuasive presence, say a prayer, and then leave. Members of faith groups have come to expect more than that. What a wonderful experience of love the family will notice when they see their minister utilize the multisensory intervention to communicate with their loved one. I have observed in recent years in the Christian ecclesiastical world that pastors relegate hospital, nursing home, and other types of pastoral care visits to other staff members. The reason given is that they have sermons to prepare and that task is far more important than the ministry of pastoral visitation. I do understand the challenge of sermon preparation as I did that for 25 years as a senior pastor. Two separate sermons for Sunday and one for Wednesday night is a task that taxes the parish pastor. So I get it. However, serving patients in hospice chaplaincy arrests my attention in that a large segment of patients have not seen their pastor, priest, church member, or other parishioner in years. I am calling for an awakening of pastoral care for parishioners with dementia. They and their families desperately need the support of the local church pastor. Adopting the multisensory intervention and teaching it to their concerned volunteers will greatly enhance the church as a place where people really are somebody even when they cannot participate in the worship and programming of the church. And I do make an appeal to parish ministers to remove the burden of financial support of the church from these people. It is taking all that the family can scrape together to provide for their loved one. Adding a burden of guilt to what they are already experiencing financially will make their journey multiple times worse.

There is also a lack of dementia care training for many hospital and hospice chaplains. I dare say that most have not had formalized training in providing spiritual care for someone living with dementia using the multisensory intervention unless they've been trained. This story will highlight the difference a trained chaplain makes in hospice chaplaincy. A long-term-care chaplain on my Chaplain Team at Cornerstone Hospice & Palliative Care received training in how to connect with patients with end-stage dementia. The training was simple on day one. Each chaplain was given a set of photographs from the "In the Garden" series of specialty photographs. The instructions were to simply show these to their patients after saying, "Mrs. Jones, I have some beautiful roses to show you." The chaplain then waited for a reaction. Each chaplain was to call me to inform me of the response of the patient. The response was great. The patients responded in various ways, but each responded. In the next session we added other nuances to the multisensory intervention and sent them out again. The responses of the patients were positive. One of the chaplains decided he wanted to excel at this intervention, so he made visit after visit and became prolific in providing spiritual care to patients with end-stage dementia. He added his own visuals as his creativity was in high gear. He also started a worship service using religious symbols that the patients could see and identify. In December 2016 this chaplain was the recipient of several cards and other gifts given to him from three different nursing facilities. The reason was simple: the leaders of these facilities had observed his ministry with their residents (also patients of Cornerstone Hospice). These leaders plus family members were overwhelmed with the level of care this chaplain provided using what we have come to call the Dementia Care Protocol.

The Dementia Care Protocol is an "above and beyond" type ministry. It is a philosophy of ministry to dementia patients. The Dementia Care Protocol lays a foundation for a very large segment of any hospice's patient population. Instead of ignoring or under-serving this large segment of patients, the Dementia Care Protocol embraces patients and works to achieve awakenings so that they may receive and respond to spiritual support.

In addition, this is the day of the family satisfaction survey. The survey is the scorecard for the hospice and its care. The chaplain can lead the way in boosting his company's survey scores. This is certainly not the lone motivator to implement this methodology, but it does have wonderful unintended benefits. It may be that the reader does not know about the Consumer Assessment of Healthcare Providers and Systems (CAHPS) Hospice Survey. There is a specific item regarding spiritual support. The primary caregiver will receive this survey within three months of the death of the patient and evaluate the services provided by the agency. The statement that evaluates the spiritual support component rates spiritual support as one of the following: Too Much, Too Little, or Right Amount. It is hoped that the chaplain will provide the right amount of spiritual support...even for patients with dementia. As an added measure to ensure family satisfaction with the spiritual aspect of hospice care, our chaplains telephone the primary caregiver after each visit indicating that the chaplain provided care using the Dementia Care Protocol. It is amazing how excited the family members are when they actually see the chaplain provide this care.

The components of the Dementia Care Protocol are: specialty photographs, music (both secular and sacred), the use of aromas, tactile objects, and affirmations of personal worth. In Chapter 4 I present a model for how to use these components. For now, just know that there is not a special order in which these are used. What follows is a testimonial of a chaplain who used the Dementia Care Protocol while the patient's spouse was present and was taken totally by surprise by what happened:

> The patient was in bed, awake, when I arrived at his room in the facility. His spouse was sitting in the chair beside him watching TV. The spouse states the patient had to be put to bed after dinner because he became restless sitting in his chair. I began providing spiritual services congruent to the Catholic faith. The patient made eye contact with me as I began praying the Lord's Prayer and he exhibited inner peace. So I took out a picture of a church building and held it in front of the patient's eyes while praying the Hail Mary. The patient looked back and forth, from me to picture, and made voices which sounded like he was trying to talk during this prayer. I could tell he was appreciative of spiritual services provided. The patient's wife was ecstatic and very grateful for my visit and was near to tears as I stood by the patient's bed and reassured him of God's ever-abiding love and presence. This is the first time this patient has reacted positively to spiritual services, today being my eighth visit with the patient. The Plan of Care will be to continue providing spiritual comfort with services congruent to the Catholic faith which will include familiar Catholic prayers. I will also take a rosary to this Catholic patient next visit to enhance his spiritual experience. (Mark Ammerman, Hospice Chaplain with Cornerstone Hospice & Palliative Care)

The benefits of the Dementia Care Protocol

A review of this chaplain's experience with the patient includes the items of the Dementia Care Protocol that were used or would be used in future visits and the difference the Dementia Care Protocol made for both the patient and his spouse. The chaplain used one of the specialty photographs of a church. Persons the age of this patient, 83, respond well to photographs of very familiar objects. This patient was a faithful Catholic parishioner prior to his ailment. The photograph triggered his memory, and he was able to attempt to join the chaplain in saying some parts of the Catholic prayers. The chaplain provided a tactile object on his next visit. The rosary is often given to patients as it triggers memories and is something of substance to grasp. Both the patient and his wife reacted positively to this experience. The patient had his positive memories stirred to the point of attempting to verbalize a prayer. The patient's wife reacted in that she had not seen him so "alive" since the condition took over his mental capacities. I spoke with the chaplain who provided this experience and his response was that this was why he does chaplaincy. This is an important statement on many levels. No chaplain should do any type of ministry if it is to do well on a family satisfaction survey. The chaplain does what he/she does because it is the right thing to do. The surveys will take care of themselves as long as the chaplain provides outstanding spiritual care. The spirit in which that note was written indicates that the chaplain is spot on with his motives. What the Dementia Care Protocol does for the chaplain and other spiritual care providers is to place a tool in their hands so they may make a difference in the lives of patients and their loved ones. Time and time again chaplains share testimonials of their work with patients and share the awakenings that occur and the responses of family caregivers to these pastoral care encounters.

The webinars and presentations that I have done have raised not only an awareness of what is possible for the patient but also of the comfort and peace it brings to the family. Having presented the multisensory intervention in various settings, it is a blessing to receive multiple emails from different locations in the country requesting further information about how to minister to patients with dementia. Family caregivers often burst into tears when they observe the chaplain using the Dementia Care Protocol with their loved one. On multiple occasions I have heard them say that what they could not do the chaplain did in such a short period of time. They are amazed at the awakenings. Quite frankly, it *is* amazing. A group of spiritual care volunteers met with me recently to ask questions about using the Dementia Care Protocol and what happens when it is used. This forum gave me the opportunity to share some of the successes chaplains have had, including my own. It boils down to a bedrock conviction that the chaplain is a catalyst for comfort and peace in a time of great uncertainty for the patient and their family. Again, I urge professional chaplains to join their parish minister counterparts to make the time to learn how to implement this approach to spiritual care and make it a priority in their care practice.

My vision for the multisensory intervention

I hope that this book will serve to inspire and educate chaplains worldwide to present the multisensory intervention to comfort and assure their caseload of persons with dementia. Further, I present this volume as a treatise to launch dementia care training in Bible colleges, seminaries, and other institutions of higher learning. Having earned two advanced degrees, I recognize the value of education that will enhance ministry. I have file cabinets filled with lecture notes of the classes I took in college, seminary, and graduate school. However, one critique I would graciously offer these institutions is that congregations are not necessarily looking for a scholar as their pastor or spiritual leader. They are looking for someone who can love them and provide pastoral care that makes a difference.

Providing a course on the Dementia Care Protocols either in the classroom or online would enhance the marketability of the graduates of these institutions. I ask the reader: "How many pastors, priests, imams, rabbis, or other spiritual leaders and guides do you know who are equipped to communicate with persons at the end stage of dementia?" Training for such a challenging ministry as dementia care is simply not on the front burner in these institutions. I'm not complaining, just urging for a change that will enhance pastoral care to parishioners. The rapid growth of the number of patients including those from faith communities calls for institutions of higher learning to provide coursework in how to provide care for these people. There are studies related to the various generations in society and how to reach them for the church. There are voluminous works on Generation X, Millennials, and the Baby Boomers. I suggest to the reader that there should be at least one volume about how to care for those already in the congregation and who are suffering from what some say is a never-ending death...dementia. I posit that it is easier to get a study group together in any congregation dealing with how culture is changing and the impact culture is having on the church than it is to conduct a study on how to express the love of God to those who no longer respond to us due to dementia. Ministry in a faith community requires an upward look to God, an outward look to find others who would choose to be a part of the congregation and an inward look to provide care to those already in the flock. Developing a balanced approach is a necessity for any congregation. I do suggest that balance is not always achieved due to many factors. For this reason, I strongly advocate for dementia care studies in the educational realm and the Dementia Care Protocol established in the local congregation. What an incredible difference this would make. The love people so often talk about to one another in the faith communities would actually mean something when the Dementia Care Protocol team knocks on the door of one its congregants and provides that loving care.

A basis for ministry

My passion for this ministry is exceptionally strong. At the very core of this passion are three moral imperatives that provide a basis for ministry to and for the patient with dementia. If there are persons whose calling it is to be moved by the needs of the vulnerable, it is certainly the clergy (inclusive of all and any faith systems). What follows are the three moral imperatives that cry out for our attention:

1. The Imperative of personhood

I have listened to family members in my Alzheimer's groups state that they feel stigmatized because their loved one lives with dementia at the end stage. No, it is not a pretty sight at times, but this is life for the most vulnerable of all human beings. I am suggesting that we review our theology of personhood. Is a person worthy of our time and attention only if they can converse with us or for what they can do for us? That seems to be the Western concept of the value of a person. Have you given thought to your theology of pastoral care? A number of years ago as I was preparing for my Board Certification as a chaplain I was required to articulate a theology of pastoral care. I explored the ministry of the Holy Spirit from my Christian background. I discovered that the roles of the Holy Spirit were to comfort, to counsel, and to companion the people of God. Those three actions sound a lot like what a chaplain does. As a hospice chaplain, I comfort people. When a family caregiver hears from the neurologist that her loved one has dementia, when she crumbles emotionally and might even cry, "No, God, no. Not his mind. Anything but his mind," I am moved to provide pastoral care. When the living nightmare of end-stage dementia has captured another patient, and they come into hospice care, I am moved to companion the patient and family. I see, again and again, the tidal wave of fear, anxiety, anger, confusion, and shock overwhelming the caregiver. Into this milieu enters the spiritual caregiver or chaplain. The chaplain has at least two persons to care for, and their needs could not be more different and the means to provide care for them could not be more different. Who is up to this task? For this reason, the chaplain needs this book to assist him or her in providing pastoral care based on proven experience. To give to someone without the least hope of receiving anything in return is the essence of spiritual care and servanthood.

2. The imperative of the caregiver

Caregivers may aptly be called saints. They provide such a level of care for their loved one with this pernicious condition that they forget to take care of themselves. In an Alzheimer's group, I often bring up the topic of self-care. Those in attendance are not in their 20s, 30s, and 40s (although they could be). Usually, those who attend the meetings are of retirement age and beyond, which means they are frail themselves. There is a common thread among the group and that is self-sacrifice. Self-care is at the bottom of the To-Do list. The Great Generation (the American generation that fought World War II) is known for its sense of loyalty.

In the case of a caregiver for a dementia patient, this sense of loyalty can be detrimental to the health of the caregiver. I recall the smallish spouse of a patient I attended. She went to work at a highly stressful job and left her spouse in the care of a person with no training in dementia care. This paid caregiver primarily fed the patient, changed the patient's adult diapers, changed the soiled sheets, and attempted to keep the patient safe. When the patient's spouse returned home from work, she took over the care of the patient. She did not have the strength to move him and injured herself in the process, but she took no time for her own care. She simply pressed on. The team of hospice staff urged her to take care of herself, but she refused. This is a common response as if the spouse/caregiver will earn the patient's healing by their self-sacrifice. Truly, this is one of the most painful scenarios in which to participate. There came a time when the patient died. One might think the spouse/caregiver went back to a less stressful lifestyle and adjusted emotionally and physically. Not so! She was left with injuries that defy healing and a spirit that is still in the process of healing. Were there other caregivers besides the hospice staff involved with this patient and spouse? Sadly, there was no one else involved except for the paid caregiver. This couple was faithful to their church, but there was no response from the church. Family members came by for brief visits as they did not know what to do to provide support. According to the Alzheimer's Association, there are "more than 15 million Americans providing unpaid care for persons with Alzheimer's or other dementias" (Alzheimer's Association 2017). The economic value of their care is estimated to be in the realm of $230 billion (Alzheimer's Association 2017). These caregivers need a voice. They need a hand. They need a heart to reach out to them in support and understanding.

3. The inseparability of the dementia patient from the common person

A dementia patient is a person just as you and I are persons. Their condition doesn't make them sub-human or non-human. They are persons who have a brain disease. Some of you reading this have a heart disorder, some a blood sugar disorder, others a breathing disorder. Does your condition make you less human? Of course not. Dementia in all of its various expressions does not deny the personhood of those living with it. I have seen dementia patients who might be described as the worst of the worst literally come alive and rejoin for a brief moment what we consider normal in terms of communicating. To suggest for a moment that a person with dementia should not receive pastoral care strikes at the core of humanness. Yes, certainly, these persons deserve spiritual care. They desperately need it. What is it like to have Alzheimer's disease or another type of dementia? Hear the words of Robert Davis. He and his wife, Betty, provide us with insight in their journal/book, *My Journey into Alzheimer's Disease*:

> Perhaps the first spiritual change I noticed was fear. I have never really known fear before. At night when it is total blackness, these absurd fears come. The comforting memories can't be reached. The mind-sustaining Bible verses are gone. (Davis 1989, p.107)

Does that not move you? It stirs within me a desire to comfort and come alongside the person with dementia. All Robert Davis held on to for comfort and peace was stripped from him by the condition. In the absence of the comfort he received from the Bible, fear took over. How sad! And yet this is the situation in which many persons with dementia find themselves.

Have you ever experienced night terrors? This is nearly an every-night experience for those living with dementia.

To further emphasize my argument why the Dementia Care Protocol will change the landscape of dementia care, dementia in all of its forms is the disease of the twenty-first century. The numbers bear me out. According to various sources, by 2050 11.5–15 million Americans will have a dementia-related condition. Currently, worldwide, upwards of 44 million people have Alzheimer's disease or related dementia. It is obvious that this condition is not going away. Therefore, it is crucial that a corps of spiritual care leaders from any and every religious system prepare themselves to provide the compassionate, understanding, and informed care that persons at the end stage of this pernicious condition need. They can be reached. My prayer is that you will become part of a growing number of professional spiritual caregivers who will take this intervention and use it in your ministry setting. This Declaration gives voice to those who can no longer speak for themselves.

Declaration of understanding and expectations

As a patient who cannot advocate for my own care, I make this declaration seeking your understanding and sharing my expectations for my care. Therefore, I declare:

- I am a person of worth; treat me as such.

- I do not expect to be treated as if I am your only patient, but I do expect that I will be given the same level of attention that you provide for persons with cancer, COPD (chronic obstructive pulmonary disease), cardiac disease, liver disease, and the many other maladies that plague humanity.

- Be patient with me. I would like to respond to you as quickly as possible; however, I simply cannot.

- Don't correct me. For the last several years, I have endured hundreds of corrections in what I've said and done. This is the best I can do.

- Don't shake me or otherwise hurt me. I know I can be frustrating. I know I can be a bother. I hate it as much as you do, but please don't physically harm me. I'm still human. I just have a complex condition.

- Play music that I knew when I was younger. Music from the 1950s is great. Church hymns provide me inner peace. Religious music from my faith group inspires me.

- Pay attention to me. I'm not dead, yet. Hold me, stroke my face, and let me know you love me. Remember, I'm here and need your loving care.

Chapter 1

The Dementias

Shall Your wonders be known in the dark?
And Your righteousness in the land of forgetfulness?

Psalm 88. 12 (KJV)

Becoming familiar with the language of dementia

The term "dementia" is used as a general description for a decline in mental ability that interferes with daily living. Dementia is not a disease as such. Types of dementia include Alzheimer's disease, vascular dementia, Lewy body dementia, frontotemporal dementia, Parkinsonian dementia, and mixed dementia. These are the most common types of what we call "dementia." The spiritual caregiver should become familiar with these terms for the purposes of understanding what is happening to a congregant or a patient on one's caseload. Regardless of the role a spiritual caregiver plays, it is vital to become familiar with the medical terminology that is used in professional discussions. I recall my early days in the healthcare environment. The discussions seemed to be in a language very foreign to me. My response to that was to take notes and look up the terms. Here is a short list of such terms that relate to dementia care:

- Agraphia—writing difficulties
- Alexia—reading difficulties
- Anomia—difficulty finding words
- Anosognosia—inability to perceive his or her illness
- Aphasia—impairment of language
- Apraxia—movement disorders
- Prosopagnosia—inability to recognize familiar people
- Simultanagnosia—inability to recognize writing and pictorial material as a whole, only recognizes the parts
- Spatial agnosia—inability to find one's way in familiar places
- Visual agnosia—inability to name or use an object without touching it

The terminology of dementia can be challenging. However, if you as the chaplain or clergy person are in a situation where these conditions are being discussed, it helps to have a working knowledge of the terms. As you witnessed, I gave short, direct definitions. Each term, however, has a rather long and detailed explanation to it. I remind the reader that spiritual caregivers and whatever roles they fill in the healthcare community are no longer in the sanctity of the faith community. The spiritual caregiver is part of the healthcare world and has an obligation to learn the language and speak the language. I have encouraged chaplains in my clinical pastoral care units to become the most informed clinicians they can. Much is at stake for the chaplain. Gaining the respect of the healthcare leaders on the interdisciplinary team or group is a major priority for the chaplain. If the physician, nurse, or team manager detects that the chaplain is a showman or comedian or other than the focused spiritual care professional, that chaplain will have difficulties. Nurses serving patients in a hospital, hospice, or other setting need someone to rely on. Therefore, I urge the professional spiritual caregiver to be as knowledgeable and conversant as possible with conditions such as dementia.

Benefits of spiritual support to the patient

I recall an instance of serving an 84-year-old female who was non-communicative in most visits. I provided spiritual support using the multisensory intervention. I showed her the "Let's Go to Church" photographs, spritzed lavender aroma, sang hymns that she was familiar with from information gained from the family, and provided affirmations of her personal worth. In this pastoral care encounter, as I showed her the photograph of the church, she experienced an awakening in which she said: "I'm in the front of the church singing." What seemed like a split second later, her facial expression went from contentment to fear. She then awakened to her terror-filled reality, saying: "They are coming! No! No! No!" I redirected her thoughts, and she left that frightening experience as I sang other more secular songs.

I spoke to the family and told them of the experience. They informed me that the "They" who were coming were several men who had brutally assaulted her over 25 years ago. They further indicated that the emotional and spiritual damage was so severe that her subsequent counseling did not resolve her sense of personal violation and that her faith, while strong, faltered as she re-lived the event throughout the intervening years of her life. As we discussed the encounter I had with her, I suggested that even in these days of her dementia, she was trying to resolve the issue spiritually. She indicated she was at the front of the church singing. That was a positive experience for her. Into that positive experience burst three evil men who still pursued her in her unconscious. She was experiencing severe existential pain which needed to be addressed. I made an appointment to discuss this case with our hospice physician. Before I met with him I reviewed this patient's chart to check on her medications. Did she have an anti-anxiety medication prescribed? There were no medications prescribed for that. When I met with the physician, I did so in bullet-point fashion. Physicians prefer that to long-winded explanations. I noted the following: The patient had Alzheimer's disease, was non-communicative except with the multisensory intervention, and was at peace until the memories of the rape entered her consciousness. My request was that the physician consider an anti-anxiety medication. There was no hesitancy on his part. He wrote the order and thanked me for the professional manner in which I approached him. Once the medication regimen was started, I noticed there was never another fearful response on the part of the patient. The medication quelled that part of her unconscious and she lived the remaining days of her life in emotional and mental peace.

I posit that the professional spiritual caregiver need always be a student. That is one reason you are reading this book. I remain a student of my patients, my staff, and of my profession. There are studies to read, research to unpack, and, most of all, interventions to use to make patients' journeys through dementia less existentially and spiritually challenging. I am a proponent of the idea that the moment we stop learning we begin to atrophy and our professional effectiveness diminishes greatly.

The medications

As we highlighted the various terms related to dementia, the professional spiritual caregiver must be conversant with the medications used to treat dementia. There are five medications on the market at this time to treat dementia. None of the five provides a cure. Each of the medications simply slows the progression of the condition. There are two medications that are used for moderate to severe dementia: Namenda (Memantine) and Namzaric. Aricept (Donepezil), Razadyne (Galantamine), and Exelon (Rivastigmine) are used in the early to mid-stages of dementia. Exelon is prescribed for early-, mid-, and late-stage dementia. The discussions you will have with the family caregivers will follow one of these routes in regard to medication:

- "I am so glad he's on (medication name)." "He is sleeping better now, or not as violent as before, or more apt to eat these days."

- "I don't see much difference in her since she started the medication."

- "He was making progress, it seemed. But, now, he is getting worse. I wish they had a medication that would cure this condition."

The medications and the caregiver

Hopefulness, disappointment, and despair describe the existential and emotional suffering the caregiver feels in dealing with medication issues. My work with patient caregivers indicates that all desire hope. Their burden of care (my words, I admit) is heavy. Just a few days ago I met a family caregiver in a store and she told me how her spouse was feeling. I was aware he has Alzheimer's disease. The hope was extinguished by the reality that his Alzheimer's had now overcome any medication and he was spiraling toward the end stage of the condition. The caregiver asked me about hospice care and what all that would mean for her and her husband. I told her of the benefits the hospice team would bring as well as the financial load being lifted with the hospice benefit of Medicare (American healthcare for the retired). We moved our shopping carts to a less-traveled aisle, so she could tell me of the challenges she faces to feed, bathe, clean, and move him. She went on to discuss the financial expenses for a home care agency and all of the medications.

The offer of a hospice is an offer of compassionate assistance with the practical aspects of life. Hospice is the cavalry! Nurse visits, CNAs, social worker, chaplain, and volunteers are wonderful reinforcements for family caregivers who are near the proverbial end of the rope. Caregivers are exhausted and need this assistance. Every country has its records of the expense of dementia. Regardless where anyone lives, family caregivers pay a toll that cannot be quantified in a monetary fashion. The terms "hope," "disappointment," and "despair" are familiar to chaplains and professional clergy. A key to enhancing the caregivers' experience is to listen and hear.

Listening and hearing

Recently, I attended a conference in which listening coupled with hearing was presented eloquently. Chaplains are trained listeners. That is the chaplain's stock in trade. This quality separates chaplains from other clergy. How many of us when conversing with a friend or perhaps another professional are more concerned with what we are going to say next or in response to the other person, or want to impress the other person with our vast array of knowledge rather than listen with hearing? Family caregivers know how to ask questions. If they want answers, they can ask questions. However, in most of my conversations with caregivers, they just want to unpack the frustrations and heartaches of caregiving. The greatest compliment ever given to me was when a caregiver said to me, "You have helped me so much today. Thank you."

What marvelous act of spiritual care did I come up with and perform? I listened. That's all. I listened. I'm sure professional spiritual caregivers have likewise heard that compliment because you listened.

Barriers to ministry

Throughout my travels presenting on this topic, I have spoken to chaplains and ministers who harbor a fear of those with dementia due the abnormality of the patients' behaviors, the lack of normality in such life skills as bathing, toileting, and dressing, and the spiritual caregiver's ability to know how to approach such patients. Perhaps the most disturbing of reasons given why the spiritual caregiver does not attempt to engage the patient with dementia is a lack of will to learn how to communicate with these persons. True, the person with dementia does not engage us in the way to which we are accustomed. True, they do not conform to our standards of interaction and behavior. However, it is just as true that they are still there...somewhere. And since it is true that they are there, it is up to us to go find them. This fact motivated me to discover the multisensory approach to provide spiritual support to this population of patients. As we apply this approach and find success in communicating spiritual support, we find that we get to look deep within ourselves and them, and engage them in their world. It boils down to our calling.

The calling to ministry

We are called to be agents of mercy and purveyors of the grace that our varied faiths offer. If that calling is only toward those without dementia, then our world is very small. As I shared in the Introduction, dementia in all its varied forms will be the disease of the twenty-first century. It is not going away.

A cure is not at hand. Medications are ineffective after a time. These persons with dementia need an incarnation of our faith. For Christians, it is an incarnational ministry of Jesus. For the Muslims, it is an incarnational ministry of Muhammed. For the Jewish, it is an incarnational ministry of Abraham, Isaac, and Jacob. For the Hindu, it is the incarnational ministry of Lord Krishna. Name the religious system and its leader and live out the virtues of that leader in relationship to the congregant or patient. It is not optional to care for those with dementia. It is the fulfillment of one's calling. I have often noted regarding my own life, "I was born to do this." The deepest desire of my heart is for hospital directors of chaplaincy and chaplains, for hospice chaplains, for spiritual caregivers of all faiths to apply the approach I am presenting, add to it your own nuances of faith, and expand upon the multisensory modalities that work in your setting. This is all for the care of the most vulnerable patients you and I will serve. The pattern I follow in introducing the dementias is to provide the medical description of the conditions and then to illustrate what these descriptions look like in a patient care setting.

Alzheimer's disease
The discovery

She sits on the bed with a helpless expression. What is your name? Auguste. What is your husband's name? Auguste. Your husband? Ah, my husband. She looks as if she didn't understand the question. Are you married? To Auguste. Mrs. D? Yes, yes, Auguste D. How long have you been here? She seems to be trying to remember. Three weeks. What is this? I show her a pencil. A pen. A purse, key, diary, and cigar are identified correctly. At lunch she eats cauliflower and pork. Asked what she is eating, she answers spinach. When she was chewing meat, and asked what she was doing, she answered potatoes and horseradish. When objects are shown to her, she does not remember after a short time which objects have been shown. in between she always speaks about twins. When she is asked to write, she holds the book in such a way that one has the impression that she has a loss in the right visual field. Asked to write Auguste D., she tries to write Mrs. and forgets the rest. It is necessary to repeat every word. (Mo 2007)

Dr. Alois Alzheimer wrote this medical note regarding Auguste D., the patient given the diagnosis of Alzheimer's disease. Dr. Alzheimer did not claim the title for this condition; Dr. Emil Kraepelin, Dr. Alzheimer's director at the Royal Psychiatric Clinic in Munich, Germany, coined the term in honor of Alzheimer's discovery.

Auguste Deter had what we now know are the common traits of Alzheimer's disease. She presented with memory problems, a sense of disorientation, and an inability to communicate and function in her world. The trajectory of her disease process led to a worsening of her condition to the point where any cognitive function failed her and she experienced hallucinations. She succumbed to the condition at the age of 55.

That she died only four to five years after her diagnosis indicates that her condition could have been active for some time prior to being admitted to the medical center. The research indicates the life expectancy from diagnosis until death is on a continuum that ranges from a few years to two decades. In the era in which Auguste D. lived there were no long-term care centers. The family provided the care. That Auguste D. exhibited bizarre behaviors at the time she was brought to the medical center indicates the family more than likely was at its wits end not knowing what to do with her. This type of exasperation is not uncommon among today's family caregivers. However, it is important to note that exasperation does not equate with lack of love. It has been my privilege to meet husbands whose wives were at end-stage Alzheimer's disease. One gentleman, a retired school board member, told me that he came to see his wife at the care center every day from 2 p.m. until the close of visiting hours, because he made a commitment to her to love, honor, and cherish her until death do they part. That is the mettle out of which many a caregiver is made. Alzheimer's disease is a complicated disease process and one that can only be completely diagnosed by way of autopsy. What begins with forgetfulness leads to confusion. Confusion, in turn, leads to aphasia. Aphasia, while not causing the following, is usually accompanied by a propensity to fall, to sit without some manner of stabilizing, and to swallow with difficulty.

> The type of aphasia seen in Alzheimer's dementia is dependent on the stage of the disorder… In the moderate to severe stages of Alzheimer's, there is a loss of fluency, increased paraphasias (use of incorrect words as well as incorrect pronunciation), and poor comprehension. (Tang-Wai and Graham 2008)

What you will experience

What this looks like in the real world of spiritual caregiving is as follows. The patient is seated in a wheelchair, often with some type of support to keep him or her secure. It is common to see the patient leaning to one side, often drooling. Because of incontinence of bowel and bladder, the patient wears adult diapers. Those with end-stage Alzheimer's disease are dressed and groomed by a CNA or family member. Their eyes may be closed, and they are non-responsive to verbal stimuli and do not engage in conversation. Some family members will state that it may have been up to a year or more since their loved spoke an intelligible word. If the patient is a resident at a long-term care facility, he or she may be in an activity room with other Alzheimer's/dementia patients where they are positioned to listen to the current activities program.

My awakening

In the early days of my work with people living with Alzheimer's, I felt helpless to know what to do in attempting to provide spiritual support. I sat next to or across from the patient wondering to myself what I was to do. My sense was that either it was me not knowing what to do or the patient not receiving what I did do. From the evening of my first day of working with those with dementia, I chose to engage in a research project to discover how I might be able to connect and communicate with this population of patients. Ignoring them or making a superficial attempt to provide spiritual support by reading a sacred text and saying a prayer were not options. There had to be more that could be done. Through conversation with other chaplains, I learned that music could be a tool to enhance the spiritual care visit. So I sang. It worked! At times the patient opened his eyes. At other times the patient mouthed the words of the song. At yet other times the patient actually sang part or all of the song. This discovery was the first step in developing the multisensory approach. The awakening, as I called it, was a great first step. I had the patient's attention but was this really enough to call it spiritual support? I did not believe it was, so I pressed on.

What I discovered was congruent with the findings of Dr. Alzheimer. In his notes, he indicated that Auguste Deter had trouble with forgetfulness, use of language, and clarity of thought at her particular stage of the disease process. I found these behaviors in the patients I served. Dr. Alzheimer provided insight into what caused these behaviors. Upon Auguste D.'s death, Alzheimer conducted an autopsy. Of note was the condition of her brain. It was shrunken and cluttered with amyloid protein. The nerves within the brain exhibited a tangled appearance.

In the halls of research today, these facts are well known. Yet, despite much knowledge, more than one hundred years have passed and there is no cure. Dementia, in all its many forms, remains a "peculiar" condition. Given that it has no cure and is affecting millions of persons, it is expected that there would be a means to calculate its severity. The Functional Assessment Staging of Alzheimer's disease (FAST) Scale was developed by Dr. Barry Reisberg (1988) and is used to designate the level of severity on a scale of 1–7 with various sub-headings. In my Alzheimer's Support Group I am often asked to describe the various stages of Alzheimer's disease. The seventh stage is for late-stage Alzheimer's disease. The impact of the condition is such that people are unable to speak well. Perhaps they can say only six words that make sense. They may repeat a sentence multiple times. They are prone to falls and need assistance walking. They lose the ability to smile and even to hold up their head. Since our focus is on communicating with patients in the end stage of the condition, the task of communicating with these persons is a daunting one. You will observe as you are providing care that by the time the patient has reached this level of severity the patient is unable to dress, bathe, and toilet independently. At this stage, the patient can no longer communicate in an intelligible manner. Some clinicians use the term "word salad" to describe attempts at speech. Whether the patient is silent or makes an attempt at speech, the spiritual caregiver will show respect, acceptance, and love to the patient. Working with people with Alzheimer's disease can be messy. Yet a theology of pastoral care must be large enough to include those with this condition. A calling to ministry is a calling to get one's hands dirty and one's nose offended by the smells of dementia, and one's eyes filled with sights that may nauseate. In Chapter 4, I share Standards of Care and Communication. When integrated into the readers' ministry style, the likelihood of communication is greatly enhanced.

Vascular dementia

Vascular dementia is the second most common type of dementia after Alzheimer's disease. About 20 percent of all people with dementia have vascular dementia. In a world that runs to quick and simple statements on just about everything, there is nothing quick and simple about vascular dementia. The term "vascular dementia" has been introduced to include the full spectrum of cerebrovascular diseases that may cause dementia. As a result, Alzheimer's disease and vascular dementia have been conceptualized as two distinct disorders that can be differentiated by careful clinical and necropsy evaluation. Traditional teaching holds that Alzheimer's disease is marked by the insidious onset of memory loss, with a slow trajectory of decline, whereas "vascular or multi-infarct dementia is characterized by stepwise cognitive decline punctuated by episodes of stroke that are accompanied by focal deficits on neurological examination, and evidence of stroke on computed tomography (CT) or magnetic resonance imaging (MRI)" (Tomlinson, Blessed, and Roth 1970, pp.205–242). Vascular dementia is caused by multiple mini-strokes. Most people with vascular dementia are unaware that something has occurred that has serious implications. The resultant damage to the brain produces an Alzheimer's-like disease process.

The caregiver and vascular dementia

Family caregivers of those with vascular dementia are cautioned about the unpredictable changes in the patient's condition. One day the patient may be doing relatively well, only to awaken the next day in a very different condition. This is attributed to the patient suffering another mini-stroke. Caregivers often express a feeling of helplessness as one mini-stroke after another occurs. Listening, empathic presence, and understanding provide what the caregivers need. While they know their loved one cannot be cured, they also need to see a way to survive the experience. The chaplain provides support that gets the caregiver through their crises.

The spiritual caregiver and vascular dementia

What should the spiritual caregiver be aware of in providing spiritual support to the person with end-stage vascular dementia? The spiritual concerns that can be observed include depressed mood, anxiety, irritability, combativeness, and indifference. End-stage patients more than likely are non-communicative. Two episodes with the same patient illustrate what can happen in a visit. This patient had had a stroke which affected his right side. His left side was very healthy. My first encounter with this patient occurred at a Veterans Salutes program. The Salutes program is a hospice endeavor to honor military veterans. It is solemn and very moving in its content and presentation. The representatives from the hospice include military veterans who serve as volunteers, a volunteer coordinator, and several other interdisciplinary team members. As we gathered by the patient's bed, the veteran volunteer began reading a letter of appreciation for this patient's service. Midway through the reading, the patient's fist punctured the letter and was punctuated with a loud grunt. As was noted above, anxiety is a characteristic of patients with vascular dementia. The patient's anxiety led to fear and fear led to a protective punch to keep the strangers away. What went wrong? Several things. First, there was a lack of communication about the issue of anxiety. This would have served as a warning for the entire group that anxiety is part of this disease process and could lead to a violent outburst. Second, only two persons at the maximum should have been at the bedside to keep the anxiety at a minimum. Third, the veteran volunteer should have been stationed on the patient's side affected by his stroke rather than on his healthy side. From this failed attempt at doing something very noble for this patient came a significant lesson learned. A Salutes event with a vascular dementia patient has not been done with such clumsiness since. The second encounter with this patient occurred when the patient was in the hospital being treated for an infection. One would think that after my experience with the patient at the Salutes event I would have stationed myself on the patient's weak side. Instead, I stood on his healthy side and got walloped. Personal lesson learned!

In a supervisory visit with another chaplain, I met a female patient with vascular dementia who would cry inexplicably. I observed that she cried when her chaplain called her name. This is not to be confused with pseudobulbar affect, however. That is a syndrome of its own. Her mood and incongruent behavior was a product of the vascular dementia disease process. This patient's chaplain provided gentle support as his voice tone and comforting words provided the emotional and spiritual support to which she could respond. Instead of singing to her, this chaplain provided soft sounds of the ocean and Caspian terns offering their unique tones. The anxiety dissipated, and the tears were quieted. The use of sounds is a nuance of music. In working with those with dementia, creativity in the selection of a tool that fits the multisensory approach is often called for.

Lewy body dementia

Lewy body dementia is the third most common type of dementia (Mayo Clinic 2018). Regardless of the rating, Lewy body dementia is a virulent disease process. It is curious that in most dementias the actual diagnosis comes post-mortem.

Lewy body dementia (LBD) is often associated with Alzheimer's disease and Parkinson's disease. The symptoms of LBD are similar to Alzheimer's disease and Parkinson's disease. I remind the reader that in hospice care we provide spiritual support for patients at the end stage of their condition. There are implications for spiritual care in two directions. The first deals with the patient. From my experience in working with patients with end-stage dementia, there is a feature of LBD that separates it from the other dementias and that is the "LBD stare." The patient's facial expression is flat. There is no emotional affect. The patient simply stares blankly. Further, LBD patients experience visual and spatial hallucinations. For instance, in my first visit as a hospice chaplain, I came upon an 86-year-old female who had LBD. I knocked on her door at the long-term care facility in which she was a resident. There was no response, so I stepped in to conduct the visit. What I observed was this patient lying in her bed, her eyes focused on something above her that only she could "see." She was reaching for whatever it was, and it appeared that she was attempting to lay hold upon it with her fingers. She was oblivious to my presence. I introduced myself several times. Since this was my first hospice patient, I was totally without guidance as to what avenue of care to follow. This was a very inauspicious beginning to my hospice chaplaincy career. However, as my research began to produce results, the implementation of the multisensory intervention became my standard approach to persons with any dementia. Thankfully, I gained insight into how to communicate spiritual concepts to these patients. The second implication of spiritual support involves the family. Family members have lived with their loved one's LBD for several years. They are emotionally exhausted from the challenges presented by LBD. "Caregivers of people with LBD experience some stressors found in other caregiving situations but also face some unique challenges that are more common in LBD" (Leggett *et al.* 2011).

From my work with caregivers in the Alzheimer's Support Group, which includes caregivers of those with LBD, it is clear that the issues that wear out the caregiver include behavioral and emotional problems, movement problems which lead to falls and injuries from such, and the fact that LBD patients resist help when offered by the family caregiver. Often a caregiver will come to the group and need to vent to the point of tears their frustration and sense of helplessness against a condition they cannot control. One morning their loved one might appear as normal as ever, only to appear nothing remotely close to normal in the afternoon. The need for more intense care of the person with LBD seemed to increase by the day. Discussing options for nursing home placement is one of the most challenging and complicated conversations a spiritual care provider will ever have with a family member. It is at this point that I must instruct the professional chaplain, minister, rabbi, imam, pastor, or priest to be extremely cautious and to allow the family member to make this life-changing decision without the religious professional interjecting statements that might be construed as guilt-inducing. To place a loved one in a long-term care setting is gut-wrenching. The family member may feel they are betraying their loved one. They feel like a quitter. They condemn themselves oftentimes for making this decision. The fact is simple: the family member cannot provide the care their loved one requires. More than likely, the family member has an injured back from lifting the loved one or the family member has developed an illness for which he or she has neglected to get care for out of a sense of loyalty to the loved one, or the family member may feel like a total failure. At this point, the professional spiritual care provider must be sensitive to the entire situation.

Another observation about the LBD patient is that he or she may suffer from contractures of the bones. Some call this cogwheeling. At the end stage of the condition, it is emotionally challenging to be present when CNAs move the patient to transport them to the bathing center. The patient is in pain as the bones and sinews have lost their elasticity. If you are the professional chaplain and the CNAs are part of your interdisciplinary team, you have a responsibility to provide emotional and spiritual support for them. I have often provided comfort for these hard-working CNAs. They are loving and gentle souls who provide excellent patient care. When they hear the patient cry out as they move the patient and hear the moans of pain throughout the bathing experience, it affects them. They need your support. I do not mean to get off track at this point. However, I am in a career that provides holistic care to the patient, the patient's family, and to the interdisciplinary team. Pastoral care embraces the total person and the total of persons providing care.

In summary, when you encounter a patient with LBD, do not be surprised if you see the patient reaching for that which is not there or when the patient looks at you with no facial affect or when the patient presents with skeletal contractures. These are all part of the end stage of LBD.

Frontotemporal dementia

This form of dementia is also called behavioral variant frontotemporal degeneration. There are hallmark symptoms of this condition which the spiritual caregiver will recognize in short order. These characteristics include alterations in their personality and outlook, indifference to life, loss of appropriate social skills, poor moral and ethical judgment, volte-face in personal habits, and a departure from their customary emotional responsiveness.

Because of the trajectory of decline observed in Alzheimer's disease, all dementias are judged by that type of steady decline. That is not the case in frontotemporal dementia (FTD). The decline is not as steady. My observation of FTD is that most patients with this condition come into hospice care with another co-morbidity. Further, most people with FTD are younger than patients with another dementia. They "look" better than other people living with another form of dementia.

At this juncture, it is important for the spiritual caregiver to recognize that a visit to the patient's home or facility might be challenging. In one experience, I was seated in the living room of the family caregiver discussing his wife's dementia. This couple was in their 50s, very religious and community oriented. The husband was telling me that regardless of his wife's condition and however long it lasted, he believed God would heal her even on her deathbed. In mid-sentence, the husband had a shocked look on his face and jumped up and ran toward the hallway where his wife was standing totally disrobed. He was embarrassed and apologized. My response was to look away and affirm that I understood what the condition was doing to his beloved wife. He took her back to the bedroom and dressed her and brought her to the living room where she sat motionlessly. This type of behavior is more normal than it is abnormal for someone with FTD. It is incumbent on the part of the professional chaplain/minister to provide the support the family caregiver needs during a difficult moment. Another encounter highlights the fact that someone with FTD can become overly familiar with a stranger—that is, you. When visiting in a memory care unit (locked unit at a nursing facility), I was visiting with an Alzheimer's disease patient when I felt a rather cold hand exploring the back of my neck. As I turned to see who was touching me, I noticed it was a resident with FTD. Behavior that would never occur in a healthy state of being now is common. The family suffers greatly as they watch their loved one deteriorate and adopt behaviors and language that they never would have used in their healthy days. When a former pastor unleashes a string of vulgarities, one realizes something is wrong. This pastor was in a nursing facility and would often scream the most vulgar of words to all who passed by his room. Family members need support from their spiritual leader. The social shame a family feels is a caregiver burden, particularly considering that the caregiver may be in his/her 40s or 50s.

Parkinsonian dementia

Statistics vary depending on the source, but approximately 75 percent of those with Parkinson's disease develop dementia. Most of us are aware of the classic symptoms of this condition: tremors, difficulty walking (more of a shuffle than taking a step), memory confusion, drooling, blank stare, leakage of urine, to name a few. My first encounter with a person with this condition was when I was a teenager. My family owned a local convenience store. I had afternoon shifts and weekend shifts. I knew about this man as he was from the neighborhood. However, I did not know the extent of his condition until he came into the store. His gait was a shuffle. His appearance featured a blank stare, drooling, and large urine spots on his pants. He could not speak clearly. All he was able to do was to grunt. Because of this, it was a guessing game as to what he wanted. I was emotionally moved as time and time again he would grunt and point to something. I could not meet his needs, which left me upset and frustrated (at myself, not him). When he would leave the store, I was left with the responsibility of cleaning up the areas where he had drooled. His presence in the store plus my inability to understand him moved me to try to devise a system that would help. The system I put together was basic. It consisted of a cardboard backing with pictures of various items on it. All he would have to do was to point or touch the object. That system worked until he no longer came to the store. His disease progression prohibited him. Serving the needs of persons like this gentleman softened my heart toward the frail elderly. I advocated for him/them in my neighborhood where they received harassment and mocking from ignorant and uninformed kids. Perhaps this was the foundation for later ministry in hospice.

It has been an observation of mine to note that when a condition has definable stages, it is very bad. Such is the case with Parkinson's disease. From my experience with these patients, I will list the stage and then illustrate what you will find as you provide ministry to these persons. I might also add that many if not all of those with Parkinson's will stay away from public settings such as faith communities. It is just too embarrassing for them and their caregivers.

Stage One is characterized by only one side of the body being affected by tremors and slight challenges in ambulating. These characteristics are often missed by family. None of the characteristics of the condition interfere with daily living.

Stage Two is characterized by more pronounced and observable worsening of tremors, muscle stiffness, difficulty completing tasks, and more obvious challenges in ambulating. The patient's balance is not adversely affected at this stage. The question may arise as to the length of time that passes between Stage One and Stage Two. There is no concrete answer. It can range from months to years.

Stage Three is the pivotal stage. The characteristics of the previous stages worsen considerably. The patient may still ambulate but with much greater difficulty. He or she may shuffle rather than walk. He or she will drool and begin to lose bladder control. These characteristics mirror those in my first encounter with someone with Parkinson's disease.

Stage Four is the stage wherein a Parkinson's patient loses his or her independence. It is no longer safe for them to venture out alone. The simple fact is they simply cannot ambulate well enough to get out of the house. They are confined to a wheelchair and often need a caregiver to move them from place to place. When one of my family members who had Parkinson's disease reached this stage, he was in a wheelchair, incontinent of bowel and bladder, required a paid caregiver, and was dependent on all his activities of daily living. He needed assistance with eating, drinking, dressing, bathing, and, as already mentioned, his incontinence. It is at this juncture that caregiving becomes a serious issue. This family was forced to have the dreadful discussion about placing their loved one in a nursing facility. In writing about the characteristics of this condition, it is necessary to identify the challenges the family members were experiencing. After a year of the disease process causing multiple physical issues, the family had to make a decision regarding placing him in a long-term care facility. At this point the family desperately needs the support of their minister. The spouse suffers greatly with a sense of personal failure as he or she contemplates the future.

Stage Five is characterized by body stiffness, hallucinations, confusion, and dementia. At this stage, the patient is usually bed-bound. The stiffness of the extremities forces this. The multisensory intervention really comes into play at this stage. Singing favorite songs relieves the anxiety so common to Parkinsonian dementia. Showing the specialty photographs triggers memories that are pleasant. The affirmations of personal worth add value to a person who has lost much of his or her sense of personhood. The impact the professional spiritual caregiver has upon both patient and caregiver/family members is immeasurable. The spouse often is overcome with a feeling of helplessness. Your presence and integration of the Dementia

Care Protocol into the visit will bring comfort to the caregiver, particularly when the patient experiences an awakening.

Mixed dementia

Just as it sounds, this form of dementia is a mix of two or more of the dementias. The extremely sad part of diagnosing this type of dementia is that it can only be diagnosed accurately post-mortem. You and I as spiritual caregivers will provide the appropriate level of care to persons who live with this type of dementia as we would do those with a singular diagnosis.

Regardless of the cause of dementia, the spiritual caregiver provides the empathetic pastoral presence, reaches out to the patient to provide loving and supportive care, and uses the multisensory intervention with expectations that there will be an awakening.

To conclude this section, I would like to recap several points:

1. The person living with dementia is still there. Their existence is in a very thick fog. They live in a world they find challenging. It is up to us to go find them in their fog using the multisensory intervention.

2. We must enter their world. We must never require them to enter our world. The condition has forever denied them normalcy and health.

3. We must prepare. Using verbal counseling strategies simply will not work. The multisensory intervention works and must be implemented as the key strategy for patient care.

4. We must be resolute in our efforts to connect with people living with dementia. Their personhood is still intact.

5. We must support the family caregiver. Their emotional, existential, and spiritual needs are great. Some are in despair, others exhausted, others deeply struggling through the disease process; yet the spiritual caregiver transfers hope, strength, and support to these angels of care.

6. While it is important to know the characteristics of the various dementias, there is no substitute for learning how to use the multisensory intervention. My opinion is that the spiritual caregiver knows some of the details of the disease processes, the medical terminology involved in discussing the condition, but nothing can replace a noble-hearted spiritual caregiver with training in the multisensory intervention who will lovingly approach his/her patient to provide spiritual and emotional care.

7. The multisensory intervention works with *all* dementias.

8. Awakenings do not happen every time, but we do not know all that happens when the songs or hymns or other religious music is played or sung, when the photographs are placed in front of the patient as the affirmations of personal worth are shared, and most of all, when love is given. It is with a sense of determination and resilience that the professional spiritual caregiver works with these patients as they are children of God who need divine support.

9. The value of the affirmations of personal worth cannot be underestimated. There is much more to be said about this later, but it was mentioned in this chapter and I want to emphasize their worth and impact.

10. Caring for the most vulnerable who wander in the valley of forgetfulness is valiant work. Supporting the families brought low by the devastation this condition has wrought is loving work.

Making a difference in these lives is divine/human work.
It is our calling…

Chapter 2

Pastoral Care Challenges

*A holistic approach to pastoral care
ministry broadens and deepens the
minister's practice of ministry.*[1]

The entire human experience comes under the purview of
pastoral care ministries. I have heard many sermons and other
addresses calling for balance in ministry. In the evangelical
world of ministry, the main concern is the salvation of the soul.
In other denominations, it is on rites and rituals. In yet other
faith communities, there is a concern for the soul connecting
to the Divine through meditation and other religious exercises.
I am calling for a practical approach to a specialized ministry
to those persons with dementia and their families. Some might
call this a niche ministry that will never get traction. To the
evangelical churches, I would suggest that you are always
seeking new ways to draw in new congregants. By providing
a dementia care ministry you will eventually win new families
as you show the value of your beliefs to the community. To the
other denominations and faith communities, I add to this that
you will live out your faith in a practical way and do significant

---

1   Author's own words.

community work as you partner with nursing facilities and other organizations devoted to dementia care.

In solving pastoral care challenges, there are three key issues: the education of professional chaplains and other clergy, the commitment to lead the congregation to support both patients and caregivers who are also congregants, and, third, seizing opportunities within the greater community.

Support for professional chaplains

We both know that most of the persons we serve on our caseloads as hospice chaplains have a diagnosis of dementia. I understand what it is like to walk into a patient's room and wonder what I will do. You need tools to use that will make a difference in the life of that patient. The Dementia Care Protocol will be that tool and will make a difference in the life of that patient and the lives of many more of the patients you serve. I have discovered in the hospice chaplain community that there is more awareness of dementia care. There are bright lights in the hospice arena as pockets of hospice chaplains are using music to provide comfort. The missing pieces for them were the same for me in the early days of my chaplaincy. Music is not the end-all. It is a means to the end of providing affirmations of personal worth and reading of sacred writings. In other words, these chaplains were on the cusp of awakenings, but do not possess a strategy of what to do when an awakening occurs. It is wonderful and something to be celebrated when any dementia patient experiences an awakening. Yet there is more that can be offered to complete the experience. This is where the Dementia Care Protocol comes into play. I will continue to provide webinars for cognate groups as requested on this subject. Further, I will offer my own webinars on this subject for those who are more than webinar viewers, but are seriously seeking to implement a ministry that will make a difference in the lives of those they serve.

Dementia care ministry in institutions of theological education

Dementia ministries, for the most part, are not on the curriculum list of institutions of higher theological learning. I spent hours reviewing the curriculum offerings of Bible colleges and seminaries and found none that offer a course in providing spiritual support to congregants with end-stage dementia. Is this too narrow a focus for colleges and seminaries? It may be, but the simple fact is that within thousands of faith communities there are families experiencing the challenges of dementia. When asking ministers about what ministry their faith community offers for these souls, I receive a blank look. The minister would ask what I mean. At that point, it is obvious that he has no idea of what I am asking. The year is 2018. Dementia in all of its forms is touching millions in America and millions more across the globe. Yet there seems to be a dearth of awareness about this in faith communities. As I reflect on the 25 years I served as senior pastor in the local church, it was clear that seminary education provided but a foundation for ministry. I attended many seminars and conferences to enhance my knowledge of how better to provide ministry to my own congregation and to the community at large.

From discussions I have had with faith community leaders, it seems that a dementia care ministry is not at the forefront of ecclesiastical ministry except for a few cutting-edge leaders. I suggest that dementia care outreach to the community at large will provide emotional and spiritual support that caregivers need.

Any attempt to address pastoral care challenges will meet with barriers. The most daunting barrier is that of knowledge and awareness. The role of the senior pastor, imam, rabbi, priest, or spiritual leader is fraught with a deluge of responsibilities. Their schedules are double and triple booked. They have to prepare sermons, studies, pastoral care visits, attend or lead committee meetings, counsel congregants, deal with internal problems, work with their staff, work with volunteers, engage in denominational or faith community meetings and conventions, plus attend to a multitude of other commitments. To add one more ministry like this may never happen. Yet I believe a dementia care ministry to the community may cause a bounce in attendance and interest in the church. We live in a day when some declare the church and other religious institutions to be irrelevant. What more could be more contemporary than a dementia care ministry? With the explosive growth of dementia across the globe, a church could make a name for itself by creating a dementia care ministry. As I have said earlier, dementia is the disease of the twenty-first century. It is not going away. The institutions charged with educating ministers cannot ignore this fact. Churches and other faith institutions cannot ignore this either as their congregants are engaged in the everyday battle against this condition.

I fully understand the challenges that dementia care presents to the local church. With most churches averaging 75 in attendance, it is hard to keep the lights on let alone provide such a specialized ministry as this. Yet a ministry to congregants with dementia and their families should rate on the scale of things the church can do. In my own experience as a senior pastor, I have fond memories of the first church I served deciding to launch a ministry to those with learning disabilities. There was one congregant whose son had such a disability. The new ministry began with him. In the immediate surroundings, there were several group homes with other men and women with the same disability. While the church was small (averaging 125 at the time), it was decided that this would be a new ministry the church would embrace. As the pastor, I participated in the work of connecting with the group homes and their residents. Many fond memories appear in my mind as I recall those great days. My point is that when the church or other faith community decides it will engage in providing care for their congregants with dementia and get the training to do so, good things will happen.

The Dementia Care Protocol and theological education

Making changes in the curriculum at a university or seminary is not an easy process. The rationale for the change needs to be unquestioned. It is a fact that leadership will determine the course of any organization. Such is the case with religious institutions. There is a two-pronged approach involved. The first prong is educating the nascent spiritual care leader in the seminary, Bible college, and other religious institutions of higher learning. The second prong reaches the active clergy of all faith persuasions. The modality used is the online classroom. This is the wave of the now. The curriculum is the same for both seminarian and active clergy. It is practical and results-oriented.

Required reading for seminarians

- *My Journey into Alzheimer's Disease* by Robert Davis

- *I'm Still Here* by Dr. John Zeisel

- and this book.

Required reading for community clergy

- *My Journey into Alzheimer's Disease* by Robert Davis

- and this book.

An investment of time and energy for both seminarians and clergy is based on worth. During my seminary days, I selected my elective studies very carefully based upon their value to my focus in ministry. As a member of the parish clergy, I was equally selective in choosing seminars that fit my focus in the church. Session one introduces the concept of dementia care in the context of ministry. Both seminarian and clergy will find this an enlightening and vital part of their ministries.

Session one—The why behind the what

The focal point of this session is to present the challenges of dementia in all its forms and how one's theology of pastoral care influences a congregation's ministries. Both seminarian and community clergy will document and present their personal theology of pastoral care and give evidence of how that influences the ministries of their current congregation. Community clergy will present a list of current ministries under the headings of Internal Ministries and External Ministries.

By talking to the families in the parish/congregation the seminarian and clergy will discover the impact that dementia has had on their lives. This will further enlighten the seminarian and clergy in that they will hear first-hand of the challenges and spiritual pain that the caregivers experience on a daily basis. Clergy and seminarian both need to not only hear this but to feel the pain. Their public proclamations will benefit from these pastoral care encounters.

Session two—The basics of dementia, part 1

The focal point of this session is to investigate the impact dementia has on the patient/parishioner and his or her family. Both seminarian and community clergy will provide case studies of their interaction with congregants with a loved one living with dementia. Questions asked are as follows (directed to the spouse or another primary caregiver): How has dementia affected you and your family members? How has the church supported you during this time? What one thing could we do that will help you through this experience? What would you like me to do for you and your family?

Having the appropriate tools for the job will enable the seminarian and clergy to effectively minister to the members with dementia. This type ministry is best spearheaded by the clergy. While the goal is to establish a ministry team to provide support for the members with dementia and their loved ones, the clergy must be lead from the front. The Dementia Care Protocol tools will be introduced and their purpose clearly presented in this session.

Session three—The basics of dementia, part 2

The focal point of this session is to discover how the seminarian and community clergy can use the Dementia Care Protocol. Each student will receive a Dementia Care Protocol kit.

Both seminarian and clergy will make pastoral care visits to memory care units in local long-term care facilities. The clergy will visit members of their parish who live in a memory care unit and seminarians will do likewise. If there are concerns about where to make the pastoral care visits, they will be resolved prior to this session.

Session four—How to make a pastoral care visit, part 1

The focal point of the discussion will prepare the class to make pastoral care visits to local memory care units to use the Dementia Care Protocol. Reporting on the pastoral care visit will include an observation, process of the visit, and what happened during the visit.

The class will review *My Journey into Alzheimer's Disease* by Robert Davis to discover some of the spiritual issues he dealt with in his experience of Alzheimer's Disease. Reviewing the pastoral care encounters in the memory care units will be juxtaposed against Davis' experiences. What were the similarities? What can be added? Reflection on pastoral care encounters is vital to perfecting the Dementia Care Protocol. Using any tool can be awkward the first time it is employed and this is also the case for the Dementia Care Protocol. Because the seminarian and clergy have experience using the Dementia Care Protocol, they will be able to mentor and encourage those just beginning to use this intervention.

Session five—How to make a pastoral care visit, part 2

The focal point of the class discussion will be the spiritual needs of the person with dementia. The minister will reflect on the challenges of spiritual care with someone who cannot respond in characteristically normal ways. The class discussion will discuss the spiritual needs of the person with dementia.

This session will focus on matters of the ego. An observation into how the clergy has become professionalized with titles, business attire or religious attire with various religious symbols reveals barriers to humble ministry to persons with dementia. The Dementia Care Protocol requires seminarian and clergy to check their ego at the door. It has been my observation that humbly serving people with dementia by singing and sharing affirmations that are short but pungent, and prayers that are brief and heart-felt make a tremendous difference to the family of the person with dementia and to the staff of the facility. Ministry is rarely done in a vacuum. The Dementia

Care Protocol will be heard and observed. The testimonials of several of the chaplains I lead will indicate the impact that the Dementia Care Protocol makes.

Session six—The multisensory intervention: The Dementia Care Protocol, part 1

The focal point of the class discussion will explore matters of the ego and how that affects ministry to people with dementia. The class will provide a brief essay on how presenting the Protocol made them feel during the visit. The ministers will make visits to people with dementia during the week.

In the twenty-first century, productivity is the operating term in business and the ministry at large. In the Western world, productivity is based upon sales made, visits conducted, phone calls made, and so on. The Western mind-set focusses on accomplishments and visible successes. That mentality will collide with ministry to persons with dementia. In this session, the class will tackle perceived failure. What is success and what is failure are important questions that must be answered. The leaders of congregation must fully buy in to the definition of success with the Dementia Care Protocol. Their ministry teams will make similar observations and will need answers based upon their leader's experiences.

Session seven—The multisensory intervention: The Dementia Care Protocol, part 2

The focal point of the class will be objections and questions. The class will unpack their experiences with parishioners and nursing home patients. Some anticipated questions/objections will more than likely focus on the fact that in some cases there was no response at all; another will focus on the lack of alertness of the patient or that the patient went to sleep during the singing, or the incredible surprise the minister experienced from the patient who responded (how did that happen?).

The seminarian and clergy will now be ready to integrate the Dementia Care Protocol into the life of their parish or congregation. An action plan will be presented with a view to implementation.

Session eight—Taking the Dementia Care Protocol to the faith community

The class will discuss creating their own dementia care ministry. The principles of creating this ministry are as follows:

- Meet with leadership—cast the vision.

- Meet with congregants caring for someone with dementia—cast the vision and listen to their needs.

- Train those who indicated they would like to learn how to use the Dementia Care Protocol.

- Assign those volunteers to their fellow congregant.

- Celebrate every awakening.

- Publish stories in the faith community social media.

- Meet with the professional media about the successes of your ministry to gain publicity for community involvement.

- Advertise for a community meeting at the faith community building. Explain what successes have occurred and open your arms to the community to provide this ministry for them.

- Train the caregivers.

- Keep the cycle going. The end result of this ministry will include a great reputation for the faith community in the neighborhood, a growing number of volunteers for the faith community, and caregivers with hearts of thanksgiving for all that has been done for their loved one and for themselves.

The class will close with a prayer to bless those who attended and their future endeavor into dementia care ministry.

What follows is a series of questions and answers that will assist you to bring the dementia care ministry to your congregants. These are questions I have responded to from presentations I have made on the topic. You may have questions that I did not include. Please feel free to contact me and pose your question.[2] I promise you I will respond as I am fully committed to this ministry.

---

2   dementiacareprotocol@gmail.com

Chapter 3

Questions and Answers

Whenever I conduct a workshop or webinar on the subject of dementia, I have a Q & A at the close of the presentation. I never assume everyone is in agreement with my conclusions or my philosophy of pastoral care. Some questions I receive have a distinct edge to them. What follows are examples of questions I fielded, with my answers. Likewise, I welcome questions from you, the reader.

1. You mentioned the professional spiritual caregiver's role in assisting families with the selection of a nursing facility. How do we do that knowing that if things don't work out, the family might blame us?

First of all, you are not to make any decision for the family. Your role is one of support. You may assist the family by gathering publicity pieces that all long-term care facilities have on hand to promote their services to patients with advanced dementia. The family's greatest need from their minister is support. In some religious systems, it is taboo to discuss placing a loved one in a facility. Experience tells me that it is easier for a non-involved outsider to condemn and criticize than to make themselves available to help the family with their loved one's care. The following are top reasons why families place their loved ones in a facility:

   a. They simply can no longer do the work it takes to care for their loved one. They have incurred injuries from attempting to transfer their loved one from the bed to a chair or vice versa. The caregiver has lost many hours of sleep caring for the challenge of sundowners. "Sundowners" is a term used to describe the syndrome of a dementia patient who has his or her days and nights confused. The caregiver must be awake during the hours their loved one is awake. As a result, normal sleep schedules are compromised. This leaves the loving caregiver exhausted and in a weakened physical state. In this condition, the caregiver is open to conditions that might go untreated due to the tyranny of the urgent with their loved one. Making the decision to place their loved one in a long-term care facility may be the only viable solution the caregiver has. It is not a decision that is made lightly. For this reason, your congregant, the caregiver, needs your support more than ever.

   b. The patient may develop what is commonly called Alzheimer's aggression. I have observed former ministers, minister's wives, and other highly religious persons curse at, hit, grab, kick, throw things at, scratch, scream at, or bite their loved one or hospice CNAs, nurses, social workers, and even me. A family caregiver can only cope with so much of this before they have to place their loved one in a long-term care facility. Critics of families who place their loved one in a facility do their backbiting and condemning from a distance. They don't see what the family is going through. In fact, if the truth were known, they don't care. Home for the caregiver can turn into a war zone. Some caregivers are injured by their loved one who explodes in Alzheimer's aggression. This is the dark side to the condition. You, as the professional spiritual caregiver, need to be aware of this. You need to know all sides of the condition so you can provide intelligent counsel. What causes Alzheimer's aggression? Like so many aspects of the condition, no one knows for certain. We can point out some reasons that may spark an outburst: fear, not knowing what is happening to them or around them, a reaction to medication, or hunger or thirst and not knowing how to communicate this need. There are military veterans who have been combative as their mind relives a frightening moment. These are all solid conjectures that will assist you as the family's spiritual caregiver to have a base of knowledge that can help the family. It should be obvious at this point in our discussion that the family caregiver needs your compassionate support. The last thing they need is to feel judged and condemned, or worse yet, to feel ignored.

2. Why are you stressing that a church or other faith community designs its own dementia care ministry? Aren't there organizations for that? Why should we bother with such an intense effort? After all, we have enough challenges filling volunteer slots for our other ministries.

Those are rather pointed questions. Let's look for common ground. First, it is true that there are wonderful organizations that provide helpful information about dementia. Some of these organizations assist with local support groups. However, a faith community has a different "feel" to it. There is a feeling of family and the emotional warmth that provides. These are elements that all parishioners need, and in our conversation about caregivers of people living with dementia it is especially true. I am troubled by the term "bother." Ministry should never be described by the term bother. If the key leader in the faith community, the senior pastor, rabbi, imam, priest, or spiritual leader cannot get behind this effort, then it is destined to either fail or be slow in developing. Those involved will grow tired of fighting what they perceive is indifference and will link themselves with one of the community Alzheimer's organizations. Losing a faithful congregant because of pastoral care indifference is unacceptable, wouldn't you agree? Building a ministry dedicated to dementia care is not easy. It will take time and work. The old adage of blood, sweat, and tears is a good description of what it will take to launch and maintain this type of ministry. Here is a plan for a year's worth of support group meetings:

a. December—Social media information posted in the second week of December. Print advertisement in the local newspaper to appear in second week of December to tie into the social media promotion. For the print ad to post in the second week in December, your volunteer for this needs to contact the newspaper advertising department in November. The print ad must contain the name of the support group, e.g. "Big Town Dementia Caregivers Support Group." The print advertisement needs to contain the location and time of the meeting, plus a telephone number for people to contact to find out more information about the group.

b. January—Initial meeting. Make it a positive, even festive atmosphere, so that people can feel relaxed. Parts of the meeting:

i. Introductions. Have a name tag for everyone. Welcome everyone warmly. Have each person introduce themselves. They will share their circumstances without prompting.

ii. Purpose of the group. The leader will share why the support group was started and what the hopes and dreams are for the group.

iii. List on the whiteboard the greatest challenges for the caregivers. This list will form the content for a future meeting.

iv. Show a brief video or have a participant share a story of their experience with any type of dementia.

c. February–December—Provide a program based on the input of those in attendance at the January meeting. Prior to each meeting, post on social media the content of the meeting. Invite community resources to share what their organization does to provide a safe environment for those living with dementia (i.e. the Public Safety Department more than likely has a program for caregivers to ensure the safety of their loved ones). Make the meetings content strong and the group will grow. There will come a time when some in the group will no longer be able to attend due to the downward trajectory of the condition process their loved one is experiencing. Do your best to connect with those caregivers to provide resources for them to use such as an adult day care or other elder care resources.

3. You prefer singing hymns and songs without using a smart phone or another device that plays the music. Why is that?

In dealing with patients with end-stage dementia, it is critical not to have clutter in what you are either showing them or singing to them. By clutter, I mean background noise—the orchestration. The melody is what they will remember; therefore, the orchestration must be removed. Do not think that you have to be a great singer for this intervention to work. That is simply not true. What communicates to the patient is your love. How you sound is not a consideration. It is amazing how the patient will attempt to sing along or mouth the words while you are singing. Perhaps you might feel awkward singing to the patient with others in the room watching and listening. I understand that feeling and came to the conclusion that the patient with dementia was the most important person in the world to me at that time and they needed my all. I worked through the awkward feeling that way. I hope you have the same experience I have enjoyed when singing to a patient in an activities type of room and as you sing a resident begins singing along with you. There is much enjoyment in this ministry. As you relax and present the specialty photographs, the hymns and songs, the spritz of aroma, and the affirmations of personal worth, and use the tactile pieces when appropriate, a feeling of deep fulfillment will wash over you. You will recognize that you have made a difference in the life of a soul.

4. I like your photographs, but I have several of my own that I would like to use. Is that OK?

Certainly, it is. From my perspective, it is expected that you will use photographs that you believe will help your patient. I simply encourage you to be sure that the photograph is of one thing only. You don't want the patient to miss what it is you are trying to show them.

5. How should I present the photographs?

This is a perceptive question. First, never quiz the patient about what you are showing them. Do not ask "Tell me what you see" or any variation of that question. Keep in mind that your patient has been quizzed multiple times over the years and is aware that he has failed multiple times. This awareness tears down the self-esteem of the patient. What this intervention does is build up the self-worth of the patient. Instead of saying "Tell me what you see," say, "This is a beautiful red rose like the ones you used to grow." Await any response. Regardless if there is a response, proceed to say, "Here is a song about a rose," then sing "In the Garden." Quizzing tears down; affirming builds up. We enter their world, which is in the land of forgetfulness, and we must be sensitive to that.

6. I am hesitant to use the spritz of aroma for fear I will use too much.

Thank you for that observation that you might use too much. The pump on the spritz bottle will release just enough of the aroma. That is all you need to use is one pump worth. Here are some further guidelines for the use of the spritz.

a. Never spray the aroma at the patient.

b. Always spray the aroma behind the patient or to the side of the patient. Spray it below the armrest of the chair or wheelchair. The potency of the aroma will permeate the space.

c. If your patient or another patient is using oxygen and has a nasal cannula, *never* use the aroma. The aroma will be directed to the patient's lungs by the flow of oxygen and cause the patient respiratory issues. Be alert before you use the aroma. Use of the aroma in my training is for the advanced chaplain/minister.

d. The spritz is designed to provide the right amount of aroma with just one press of the pump. One press of the pump is all you need.

7. I am getting frustrated. Nothing seems to work.

I have been there, experienced that. In the Western culture, we are results-oriented. We want a "big bang for our buck." That philosophy will crash and burn using the multisensory intervention. There are days when nothing works. I remain inspired by the Catholic patient who did not respond to any religious song I sang. However, when I sang "Santa Claus is Coming to Town," she responded. My encouragement to you is press on. There will be a visible awakening one day. My understanding of ministry is that I am but a vessel to bring a blessing. I do not work alone. I have a divine Companion who walks with me into the homes I visit and the facilities I visit. I trust that my efforts will not be wasted because God is my Helper. I believe He will take what I do and provide comfort and peace to the patients I serve regardless of whether they show an awakening. I believe the bodies of some of these patients are so weakened by the condition that they simply cannot respond in a physical manner. Nearly all ministers have heard that the last sense to go is that of hearing. I accept that as well. If that is the case, then I will continue to sing, to provide affirmations of personal worth, and provide brief and poignant sacred readings and brief and poignant prayer.

8. Follow-up question... You just mentioned prayer. How do I pray?

The temptation is there for all ministers to provide a long, theologically sound prayer much like what the minister would pray in the faith community setting. That won't work with a dementia patient. The prayer, the blessing, or the sacred reading must be brief. A sentence or two using common words is the best prescriptive I can provide. It may seem shallow or ineffectual, but keep in mind the patient cannot stay with you for long due to the condition. If your patient has an awakening, proceed to a brief sacred reading, blessing, or prayer. The window is obviously open. Your words will be heard. Comfort and peace will enter the heart of the patient.

9. You gave an illustration of echolalia. Can you say more about that?

Let me review this phenomenon again. Some patients with frontotemporal dementia will express echolalia. It looks like this:

a. The patient is seated, rocking back and forth repeating a number of rhyming words or several different words or a phrase.

b. The question is often asked, "Why?" It could be an expression of anxiety or of some other troubling emotional feeling. Our task with this patient is the same as it is with all other patients and that is to provide an empathetic pastoral presence and provide the multisensory intervention which will bring comfort and peace to the patient.

c. What do you do? First and foremost, keep your wits about you. Don't react to this behavior. Respond to it gently and compassionately. Listen to the words. How many are there? As you listen to the patient, recite this group of words over and over. Which word is the first and which is the last on the list? Does the list of words make sense? For instance, I came upon one of my patients in the midst of an episode of echolalia. As I listened to the list of words, I determined which was first and which was the last. My thought was that if I slip a new word that had spiritual meanings to it, I might provide the patient with comfort. Because the patient was Catholic, I said the beginning of the Hail Mary. The patient took it from there and created a new list of words: Mary, Mother of God, Jesus, pray, sinners. It is my belief that persons expressing echolalia may be attempting to deal with their internal spiritual stressors to close the loop on their earthly lives. I do not see echolalia as something to be afraid of or to be avoided. As ministers and chaplains work with patients and congregants without dementia, we are aware that tying up the loose ends of life is a major task. Echolalia may serve as a cue to the chaplain that the patient needs comforting sacred readings and prayers to reduce anxiety.

10. How do we have a worship service at the memory care unit?

There are a number of steps to take to initiate a worship ministry. One of the key elements is the time for the worship program. Dementia patients are usually more alert in the morning. They often nap in the afternoon. If you select Sunday as your day for worship, you, as the spiritual leader for your faith community, will have to make a decision to allow a team of your laity to miss the regular worship service at your church. If you select Saturday or even a weekday, you might avoid controversy. Preparation is the next greatest challenge. Symbols are very important in the worship experience. Patients may respond well to the sight of a Bible or other sacred text. They may respond well to the sight of a model of a church.

If yours is a Christian church, you will want to select very well-known hymns. There is no need for an instrumentalist as the person singing will use his or her voice to convey the melody of the hymn. Likewise, if yours is a Jewish, Muslim, or other religious system, there is no need for instruments. This program of worship will be brief and will be patient-centered. The goal is to provide a meaningful experience for the patients. "Platform decorum" is unnecessary. You, as the worship leader, and the person doing the singing will mingle among the patients so you are close to them. This is not a traditional worship program. This type of program is work for the leaders. Connecting with the dementia patient in his or her world is not easy, but can be done. You can take the model of the church/synagogue/mosque with you as speak. Key themes to your presentation: You are safe, God loves you, God cares for you, I love you, I care for you, You are special, You matter, You matter to God, You matter to me. Build a brief three- to four-minute presentation around any of those affirmations. Whatever you do, do not use complicated theological constructs in your presentation. Use the specialty photographs. Do not feel that you need to come up with a different presentation every week. The needs of the patients are primary. Their needs include belonging, love, sense of safety, peace, worthiness, security, to name a few. Those who are part of your team will introduce themselves to the patients prior to and after the program. They will say, "My name is Rich. I am glad to be here today. I care for you." The program itself will take about 15–20 minutes. Afterward, your team will take a set of photographs and meet individually with patients and show them the roses or the religious photos. Your team will show the photographs, sing hymns or songs that connect with the patient, use the affirmations, and have a brief prayer. Your team will have done a great service for these patients. Your reward will be special.

The above can be adapted to any other religious system. It is pretty clear that human connection is primary. That will speak louder than any sermon or homily. These people need the human touch. Your team will provide that.

Having served as a senior pastor for 25 years, I learned that the lay people want to do something of significance. A dementia care ministry will provide that platform. As their leader, you will train them for this ministry. The type of person you want on your worship team should be someone who seeks to serve and not someone who expects results. The joy is the serving. The celebration is the awakening. Serving is guaranteed. Awakenings are not. The patients are living in a world they find challenging and need someone to show them the way out. This is the awakening. These experiences are special. They do happen, sometimes often, sometimes not often. Being with the patient will go a long way to make them feel special and loved.

Chapter 4

The Power of Presence

Only God knows the difference we make with people with dementia. We never give up on our efforts to connect with these precious souls.[1]

As I review my experiences with patients, I've come to understand the difference between being and doing. I often took a hymn book with me and sat next to the patient's bed and sang several hymns and then sat quietly for a few minutes. People living with dementia need time to attempt to process the songs. I then shared several affirmations and spoke them slowly and distinctly. There is no question in my mind that this led to many awakenings. Your presence carries power, the power that connects to the patient. This is the essence of presence. I recognized that I was a fellow traveler on this journey of life. My patient was someone who needed me on their journey. Acceptance, love, companionship were qualities of my life that I shared. May your experience in this ministry fulfill your calling as it has done mine.

The following testimonial from one of my Chaplain Team is as inspiring as it is educational. Orlando Rodriguez employs the Dementia Care Protocol with passion and precision.

---

1   Author's own words.

"Please don't hurt me" was the expression of one of my dementia patients on one of my initial visits. Today that expression remains in my mind, it makes me realize how important it is for a dementia/Alzheimer's disease patient to feel safe, and how vital it is for me to communicate with them and connect with them at their level. I was always aware of the spiritual and emotional needs of my dementia/Alzheimer's disease patients, but communicating with them through regular means was not making any sense, regular conversations with them were almost impossible, getting a response was a challenge on every visit, I knew I was not meeting their needs. If I wanted to create a "safe place" where they could laugh, sing, experience joy, and express their emotions freely, I needed to learn to communicate with them in a language they could understand.

I am from Puerto Rico; my native language is Spanish, and it took some time to learn English. I have an idea how it feels to be surrounded by people talking in a language you do not understand, and how it feels to be around many people and still feel lost because you cannot communicate or relate to them. Having a person that could communicate with me during that time was like "finding an oasis in the middle of the desert." When the Dementia Care Protocol was introduced to me by my Spiritual Care Manager, Rich Behers, I immediately realized the significance of this concept and started implementing it. The Dementia Care Protocol allowed me to "learn the language" to communicate with my dementia/Alzheimer's disease patients at their level. After I started implementing the Dementia Care Protocol with my dementia/Alzheimer's disease patients I witnessed that many of my patients who didn't talk, smile or show emotions for many years were now responding, talking, smiling, singing, experiencing joy, and expressing emotions. On one occasion, I visited a patient diagnosed with Alzheimer's disease. She always appeared to be depressed, sad, and was mostly nonverbal. I learned she used to be a hairdresser and that she loves flowers. I printed several pictures of hairdressers and the pictures of flowers and had them ready for my next visit. On my next visit with the patient, I sat down with her and using the Dementia Care Protocol I showed her the picture of a hairdresser fixing a woman's hair and the pictures of flowers. The reaction was magnificent: for the next few minutes she was the happiest person in the unit, grabbing and looking at the pictures, smiling and saying, "I like it" and "I like flowers." At the end of the visit I started singing the hymn "Amazing Grace," and to my surprise she sang the entire hymn with me. The facility staff was amazed because they hadn't witnessed this patient responding this way since she was admitted. On another visit I sat next to a patient diagnosed with cerebral degeneration. For months she had been nonverbal, lethargic, always keeping her head down. I held her hand, provided a word of affirmation, telling her "you are safe," and she responded, squeezing my hand, then leaning on me and putting her head on my shoulder, and said, "You made me feel safe." For me, the Dementia Care Protocol is the channel to meet the spiritual and emotional needs of dementia/Alzheimer's disease patients; making them feel safe through affirmation, creating moments of joy with pictures and music, and facilitating the free expression of their emotions.

The beauty of the Dementia Care Protocol is that it is not restricted or limited to a one-to-one encounter with a dementia/Alzheimer's disease patient. I have been able to expand the Dementia Care Protocol to group settings and celebrate religious services for my dementia/Alzheimer's disease patients using religious symbols. I regularly place a church replica on the table to bring them to church, a black Bible to let them know I am talking about the Word of God, and a battery candle to symbolize Jesus is the light of the world. Using these symbols through the Dementia Care Protocol has allowed me to create a church environment that makes sense for the dementia patients. Again, the beauty of the Dementia Care Protocol is that it can be applied to all faiths and religions using their symbols. Through the Dementia Care Protocol, I discovered a new passion: to provide spiritual care to dementia patients. I am in the process of expanding its use to persons with mental illnesses and I am having similar results. (Orlando Rodriguez, Hospice Chaplain with Cornerstone Hospice & Palliative Care)

Orlando and I have had many conversations about the benefits of the Dementia Care Protocol, not only for patients but also for the chaplain. My assessment of his pastoral care skills has always been that they are good; however, in his own words, he has "found a new calling" and that is to provide spiritual support through the use of the Dementia Care Protocol. Perhaps you too will discover a new dimension to your call to serve God. That is my hope and prayer.

Your Dementia Care Protocol toolkit

The multisensory intervention has the following elements:

- The specialty photos.

- The aromas. Please be sure you use the scents properly.

  - Rose scent: this is your main scent

  - Pine scent

  - Chocolate chip cookie scent

  - Lavender scent: use this for the patient exhibiting anxiety.

- Music

- Sacred: Do not feel a need to use all of these hymns in any single visit. Use what the patient is familiar with. Create your own list of sacred songs from your own faith system. Do not feel that you have to use all of the stanzas of the sacred songs. Often, I would repeat the first stanza several times so the patient could grasp the content of the piece. Also, sing them slowly and never rush through the songs.

  » "Amazing Grace"

  » "Jesus Loves Me"

  » "Ave Maria"

  » "It is Well with my Soul"

  » "How Great Thou Art"

  » Seasonal hymns.

- Secular songs

- Children's songs are often effective in gaining an awakening for the person with dementia. Review the list of children's songs. Which one(s) do you think the patient will enjoy? Keep in mind that the patient may enjoy other genres of music. If one style of music does not have an effect, try another. Do not limit yourself in your musical selections. Perhaps one of the children's songs listed below will trigger the patient's memory:

  » "Jack and Jill Climbed Up the Hill"

  » "Twinkle, Twinkle Little Star"

- » "Mary Had a Little Lamb"

- » "Old MacDonald Had a Farm"

- » "Hickory Dickory Dock"

- » "London Bridge is Falling Down"

- » "Rock a Bye Baby"

- Popular songs from the 40s, 50s, and 60s can trigger the memory. These can either be sung by you, the caregiver, or played on a device:

  - » "You Are My Sunshine"

  - » "That's Amore"

  - » "A Bicycle Built for Two"

  - » "Singing in the Rain"

  - » "America the Beautiful," and other patriotic songs.

- There are many more songs from which to select. Caregivers know their loved one and his or her favourite songs from yesteryear. Make the patient's room at the memory care unit a place of song. The patient will benefit from the positive impact of music.

- Affirmations of personal worth. Review these to the point that you do not have think about them, you just say them. When saying these to patients, be sure your voice tone conveys warmth and sincerity.

- Tactile objects: I recommend military patches and rosary sets.

- Symbols: To use in worship services as well as personal visits.

  · Model of a church

  · Model of a synagogue

  · Model of a mosque

  · Bible, Koran, Torah, sacred writings from your faith community.

From experience in making visits in long-term care facilities, I always take a small folding stool for the simple reason that most facilities do not have chairs for visitors to use. You will need this when making your visits and conducting worship on a one-to-one basis.

Prayers
For the chaplain and ministers of all faiths
Lord of life, thank you for those who have read this work. My prayer is that they would catch the vision of what could be for patients with dementia. Bless them with passion and love. May their efforts issue forth in awakenings, so that they may share affirmations of personal worth and spiritual messages that will minister to the patient. Bless them, also, with resilience and determination. When they make their way back to their homes or offices, may they feel a deep sense of inner satisfaction knowing they made a difference in someone's life. Amen.

For faith communities
To the God who calls faith communities to embrace one another, I ask for the leader a blessing of vision for a dementia care ministry. May his/her passion birth a ministry

for caregivers and for patients. May he/she seek out training for the congregation and may the trained go forth to provide spiritual care for the patients. May caregiver support groups develop and carry forth a message of hope and encouragement. Bless congregations that care enough to do ministry for this vulnerable population within the faith family. Amen.

For institutions of theological and ministry education

O God, the Creator of the mind, bless the leaders of these institutions with great vision to see the difference their students will make using the Dementia Care Protocol. Give them the courage to launch a program which will instruct and inspire their students. Give them eyes to see, ears to hear, and hearts to feel the challenge of dementia care ministry and act upon it. Amen.

A general prayer for those with dementia

God, you see your children challenged with dementia, fearful, and in need of care. It is our prayer that you would comfort them and meet the deepest needs of their lives. Our prayer is that you would send to them compassionate spiritual care workers to apply this Protocol that they may experience awakenings and therein experience the comfort of your peace. Amen.

Chapter 5

The Multisensory Intervention

If you plan to reach out to people living with dementia, here is your best intervention to do so.

The term "multisensory intervention" sounds sterile and isolated. However, this methodology or intervention is part of a philosophy for communicating with patients with dementia. This philosophy is called the Dementia Care Protocol. From the previous chapters, you will have gained insight into the passion and dogged determination the spiritual caregiver employs to connect and communicate with the patient. Therefore, the elements of the Dementia Care Protocol include attitude, perceptiveness, and skill.

Regardless of how many years of experience a pastor, priest, imam, rabbi, or other spiritual care official may have, in dementia care attitude is everything. I can teach the principles and procedures of the multisensory intervention, but if the attitude of the spiritual caregiver is nonchalant toward dementia care, then all will be for naught. This ministry is one of skill and will. There is a skill to using the various elements of the multisensory intervention, but also the will must be present in the heart of the spiritual caregiver to persevere through the ups and downs of ministry to dementia patients. The attitude the spiritual caregiver possesses toward dementia patients will determine the level of care he/she will provide the patient. This is not easy work. It is not sitting across from someone who can communicate. It is attempting several different options to make a connection with a patient living with the condition of dementia. There are days when nothing works and there are days when most everything works. One's emotions are always expressed through body language and intonation of language.

Body language

It is a principle of human relations that body language reflects our inner attitude. Body language is the silent aspect of communication. By way of example, I recall a training session I had with a relatively new chaplain. I observed his style of listening to patients and family members. He sat on the edge of his seat and leaned forward and looked intently at the patient. This is a very intimidating posture. The level of communication with this non-dementia patient was nil. I spoke to him about this, and he explained that he wanted to appear totally committed to listening to the patient. He was not aware of the basics of body language. When our personal space is invaded, communication is stifled. A distance of at least three feet is a safe space for communicating serious messages. Having a relaxed posture enables the patient to feel relaxed. Having a tight, tense, terse look will not assist the spiritual caregiver in communication. If these principles are true in attempts to communicate with healthy people, it is even more so in communicating with patients with dementia. Keep in mind: patients living with dementia can find life challenging and stressful. Approaching patients with a calm, easygoing body language will greatly assist your attempts at connecting and communicating. Smiling and facial expressions greatly enhance your pastoral presence. Keep in mind that a dementia patient needs to feel safe. You are a stranger to that person regardless of how long you have known them. Their brain has a condition that disrupts memory. Taking for granted that the patient knows you is a bad assumption. Smiling disarms people in general and communicates safety. Smile a lot when you are with your patient. I am not blessed with a "soft" face, so I must work at this especially hard. Here are some exercises to help soften your look. Work at raising your eyebrows. Raised eyebrows can convey surprise. That's not the look you want to attain. Raising the eyebrows slightly opens the eyes and, for that matter, your entire face. That is the look you want to attain. Sit before a mirror and do this exercise. First, present your "normal" face. What are you conveying with your eyes? Your mouth? Your cheeks? Your forehead? Your eyebrows? Each of these facial components is vital in how you are perceived by people. A furrowed brow exudes impatience. A frown conveys unhappiness with the task at hand. A mouth that turns downward conveys disappointment and even anger. Eyes that squint indicate difficulty with vision, pain, or lack of understanding. There is nothing good about any of these facial components and they will turn off or cause the patient to sleep or drop their head to their chest with a sense of disconnect with you. I encourage you to practice softening your facial expressions several times a week. In addition, do a self-check on your body language. Too many times I have been asked, "Rich, are you OK? You look upset/angry/too intense…" I speak from experience and urge you to learn your body language.

Your arms also communicate strongly to patients. The goal is to position our arms so that they do not communicate rejection or impatience. Be certain you are aware when around dementia patients that your arms are not crossed. An undisciplined spiritual caregiver who presents with a frowning face or a scowl and has crossed arms is not going to have success ministering to patients. Let your arms fall gently to your sides. When you move your arms as you are talking to the patient or singing to the patient, have your arms help you do the talking or the singing. Open them as if to embrace the patient. Hold the patient's hand; look them in the eye with soft eyes. You will be amazed at how well your visit will go. A word of caution is needed at this point. Should you decide to hold the hand of the patient, and you are a male chaplain, be sure to place your hand under the female patient's hand. The rationale for this is to give the patient the power to take her hand away from yours. Male chaplains should never place their hands on top of the female patient's hand. Doing so communicates to the patient that you are in control of her. There are so many obstacles to overcome in end-stage dementia ministry that you don't need to add to list by exerting control over the patient.

Your torso also conveys a gentle approach. Never sit on the edge of your chair with your torso stiffened, pointing toward the patient. If you are sitting, do so with your body relaxed. A stiffened torso adds chaos to an already chaotic environment for the patient. Keep in mind that by the time a patient has reached the end stage of dementia, they have had many people convey impatience and frustration to them with a torso pointed toward them with an outstretched hand and pointed finger. That is not the style of a chaplain or other spiritual caregiver. Our role is to be gentle, welcoming the patient into our space. Excellent body language lets the patient know you are willing to take a journey with them in their world.

A good practice before you enter a home or facility where your patient lives is to pause before you knock on the door or enter a memory care unit and take a deep breath and blow the air out as if to symbolically exhale the tension and stress you are feeling at the moment. Take a deep breath and plunge into your visit. Our goal is always to prevent the patient from knowing that our world is chaotic. Chaos plus chaos equals no communication. That's not much of a mathematical equation but it conveys the point. Your inner attitude of love for dementia patients has the chance to come forth as you introduce yourself to the patient. Your smile, your intonation, and your body language say to the patient in an unmistakable fashion, "I am glad to be here with you!" before you even say a word.

Introducing yourself to a person with dementia

The Dementia Care Protocol requires a positive initial contact. To reiterate, this is as much a philosophy of ministry as it is a means to communicate with dementia patients. The groundwork must be well laid by the spiritual caregiver. One cannot just enter a room, show pictures, sing a song, spritz aroma, and be done. The spiritual caregiver choreographs the visit. Why? The damage this condition has done to the patient is such that there must be multiple parts of this Protocol to ensure an excellent visit. The first part of the visit is crucial then for what follows.

When speaking to the patient, it is imperative that your voice be your normal speaking voice. Enunciate each word properly. When you enter the patient's room, feel free to sing your introduction. For those from a Christian background, the last phrase of the hymn "Jesus Loves Me" provides an effective way to sing your way into your patient's room. The words you would use are these: "Hello, Mr. Jones. Hello, Mr. Jones. Hello, Mr. Jones. This is Chaplain Rich." Practice this approach when you enter the room and you will see it can be very effective in setting the tone for the meeting. You are smiling, your voice has set the tone for the visit, and now you are ready to communicate with your patients.

Specialty photographs

The parts of the multisensory intervention are specialty photographs, aromas, affirmations of personal worth, tactile objects, and symbols. As I developed this intervention, it was clear to me that it had to be multisensory because of the damage that was done to the brain by the condition. Conversational visits could not happen. Awakenings were the goal. How long the awakening lasted was and will always be secondary to the awakening itself.

A major part of the multisensory intervention is the catalog of specialty photographs. You have read several times in this book about "specialty" photographs. What makes them special? Simply put, these photographs are of one thing only. As I began my research into how I would build a system to communicate with patients with dementia, I read many articles and books that dealt with communicating with patients with early or mid-stage dementia. Some clinicians used pictures cut out of magazines to communicate with their patients. This seemed to work for those patients. I used this approach with end-stage patients and discovered it was a total failure. Patients at the end stage of this condition cannot focus upon small images in the midst of other small images. For instance, I tried to show a patient an apple in a fruit stand with multiple types of fruits. After the first glance, the patient looked away. I met a wonderful photographer, Carol Gilmore. She has a heart for dementia patients and had a desire to do whatever she could to enhance my efforts to develop a system that would work. We met and I asked her to take photographs of one thing only…one rose, one animal, one flag, one eagle, etc. The point was to minimize the background clutter so the photograph could magnify the object. These photographs were printed on standard-size paper in brilliant color and laminated.

Laminating the photographs with 7mm laminating pouches made them sturdy and long-lasting. There are times when a patient will want to hold the photograph to look at it intently. The spiritual caregiver need not try to reclaim the photograph if the patient has made it hers. The photographs are easy to reproduce and laminate. It is better to print off another photograph than wrestle it from the patient. Another reason for using the 7mm lamination is that it allows for cleaning of the photograph. One thing that is always of concern in healthcare is infection control. Wiping the laminated photograph with a spritz of 1:10 ratio of bleach to water will prevent the spread of bacteria from one patient to another, let alone from the patient to you, the spiritual caregiver.

The photographs come in a catalog. They are available to all who purchase the book. The photographs in the catalog include: At the Beach, At the Synagogue, At the Zoo, Bath Time, At Church, In the Garden, and Snack Time. New photographs will be added continuously. You might want to pause in your reading to look at the photographs. Since you are new to using these photographs, here is a step-by-step tutorial on how to use them:

Step one
Download the photograph and size it using your computer's tools to cover a standard 8.5 x 11 inch sheet of paper.

Step two
Laminate each photograph with a 7mm laminating pouch. Depending on your employment situation, getting this done might take a day or so. Volunteers in hospice and hospitals deeply desire to be used to assist chaplains. Allow them to do this task. If you are a spiritual leader in a local faith community, you might need to purchase a laminating machine and a box of

7mm laminating pouches. Be sure you use the 7mm pouches; anything smaller will cause the photograph to crinkle and be very difficult to use.

Step three

Select patients to see. The best time to visit dementia patients is in the morning. After lunch, they will nap. You do want to see them when they are most alert.

Step four

Decide which songs you are going to sing. "You Are My Sunshine" is a proven song to start a visit. If you use the "In the Garden" photographs, select the hymn "In the Garden" to sing when you show the patient the photograph of the red rose with dew drops on it. CAUTION: Do not ask the patient if he or she sees the dew drops. Simply say, "I have a rose with dew drops on it. It reminds me of a beautiful song…" Then sing "In the Garden." Often, patients will either mouth the words or sing a few words as you sing. Do not be in a rush to complete the song. Sing slowly and distinctly.

Step five

If you are visiting a patient in the memory care unit of a facility, you must ring the doorbell or another device to get the attention of the facility staff to open the door to allow you entrance. You will also have them let you out of the unit when you complete your ministry.

Step six

Now that you are in the memory care unit, you must find your patient. The staff will be happy to assist you with that. If the patient is in the common area of the unit, the staff member will ask if you would like to see the patient there or in the patient's room. Depending on the level of distraction where the patient is, I would visit the patient in the common area. There are two reasons for this. First, it causes less stress for your patient. He or she is already comfortable sitting where he is. Second, your presentation of the specialty photographs and singing will touch the other patients as well as your own. It has been an amazing thing for me to sing songs and hymns and note how many other people in a memory care unit will respond to them. If you opt to visit the patient in his or her room, always leave the door open. Anytime there is a male spiritual caregiver visiting a female patient, doors need to remain open. That principle applies also to female caregivers visiting male patients. I might add that there are religious mores that you need to be aware of. Families of Jewish patients and Muslim patients will appreciate your adherence to their gender guidelines.

Step seven

You have found your patient! Mr. Jones is in the common area of the memory care unit of the facility. The atmosphere is calm with little confusion. You decide to conduct the visit there. Now is the time for a supportive and positive salutation. Key facts about Mr. Jones:

- He does not speak.

- He is a World War II Veteran.

- He has Alzheimer's disease.

- He presents in a wheelchair and leans to his right side.

"Hello, Mr. Jones. Hello, Mr. Jones. Hello, Mr. Jones. This is Chaplain Rich" (sung to the tune of the last line of "Jesus Loves Me"). Allow the patient a moment to let your greeting to resonate. Your next words need to be positive about the patient's looks or response. "Mr. Jones, you look good today." (It is my assumption that the patient is non-responsive and seated in his wheelchair.) "Mr. Jones, I have a couple of very nice pictures about America." You place the photograph of the flag of the United States of America close to him, so he can see it and sing the national anthem. Depending on his response, you show him the photograph of the bald eagle, the national bird of the United States. You sing "America the Beautiful." Again, you await his response. If there is not an awakening, then proceed by placing the military patch representing his branch of military service in his hand and thank him for his service. The goal of using the multisensory intervention is to create an awakening which can be as simple as raised eyebrows, a meeting of eyes, or in this case caressing the military patch. As this military veteran caresses the patch it appears as if he is trying to re-create memories from his military days. He then held the patch with both trembling hands and looked closely at it, he then raised one hand and offered a salute. That is an awakening! Upon the awakening, I shared several affirmations of personal worth: "Thank you for your service. God loves you. God cares for you. You are safe."

Earlier in the book, I wrote about the matter of prayer. Many religious systems and denominations have long prayers for those with a condition such as dementia. In this case, brevity is the operative word. Simply pray, "Thank you, God, for Mr. Jones. May he experience your love today. Amen." Of course, your prayer for a blessing upon the patient is up to you but the example I gave depicts the brevity of the prayer. The patient in the midst of an awakening can know what you are praying when it is brief. You don't want to lose the patient in a plethora of words. After the awakening, the patient reverts to a non-responsive state. My practice was to stay with the patient for 10–15 minutes after the prayer. I would sing on occasion or read short Bible verses until the patient dozed off to sleep. Further, it was my practice to bless the patient with my hand on his or on his shoulder. Since this is your first experience, you may feel awkward singing or showing the patient the photographs. That is normal and natural. You must push through that to minister to the patient. Do the best that you can with your first patient and don't expect too much of yourself.

Step eight: Review

After your first experience, you may need to get alone and take a deep breath from the anxiety that may have built up inside. Take time to review the experience. What did you feel good about? What would you change? Keep in mind that you will be making hundreds of visits to dementia patients. You will find the rhythm of the visit. You will move from robotic to smooth. You have taken the first step to a ministry of meaning-making for dementia patients. Congratulate yourself!

Aromas

Aromas are another piece of the multisensory intervention. Before I write anything else about the aromas, I urge caution in using them. Many of you will be serving patients in long-term care facilities, meaning there will be patients and other residents using oxygen. Therefore, it is absolutely imperative that if your patient is using oxygen you refrain from using the aromas as they are very strong (out of necessity) and would be forced into the patient's lungs. That could cause significant problems. So, I emphasize: never use aromas with a patient who is using oxygen or when you are around patients using oxygen. With that said, the aromas add a wonderful ambience to the visit. When you are using the "In the Garden" series of photographs, the rose scent is beautiful and will assist to trigger the patient's memory. I have seen this happen many times. When you are using the "Snack Time" photographs, the chocolate chip cookie aroma has a similar effect. I do not craft these aromas but use an online company for purchasing them. The website saveonscents.com provides a list of hundreds of aromas. These are not cheap, knock-off aromas. I urge you not to use fragrances you might purchase at a discount store. They do not suffice for what we are trying to achieve. As you have observed by this time, the photos and the aromas are to be unmistakable in their visual and olfactory impact. When using the aromas, always spritz behind or below the patient. Never spritz the aroma at the patient's face or body. If need be, you can fan the aroma once it is spritzed. Experience will reveal that fanning the aroma is mostly unnecessary. The purpose of the aroma is to trigger memory. With the specialty photograph, the purpose is to trigger the memory of what a rose looks like. More than likely, the patient hasn't seen or handled a rose in a considerable period of time. For this reason, I stated that if the patient desires to hold on to the rose photograph or any other photograph, let them have it and make another. With the photographs and aromas, we are attempting to move the patient's memory to a time past. To trigger those memories that have not been totally affected by the dementia is our goal. Adding to this effort is music.

Music

Music is enjoyable and fun. The music we use can be described as heart music and relational music. The heart music includes the hymns and sacred songs that the patient enjoyed in days of health. An amazing fact is that there is a part of the brain that defies dementia and holds tightly to the sacred. Could that be a work of God? I am convinced it is. If the patient is from a faith background other than Christianity, I urge a consultation with the local rabbi, imam, or Hindu or other spiritual leader to gain insight into the music and sacred reading that might trigger the patient's memory. Collaboration with community clergy is a required element of professional chaplaincy. When you collaborate, always document the conversation in your company's electronic medical record.

Familiarity is what we are trying to achieve with the music. Because of that, you do not have to a repertoire of 20 or more hymns or songs. A few suggestions here would include:

- "Jesus Loves Me"

- "Amazing Grace"

- "It Is Well With My Soul"

- "You Are My Sunshine"

- "America the Beautiful"

- "A Tisket A Tasket"

- "Home, Home on the Range."

The best source for music is the patient's family. They will tell you the type of music their loved one enjoyed. Take their suggestions and teach yourself the songs and enjoy your time with the patient. You will be surprised at the number of awakenings your patients will experience. Your efforts will open the door to allow a powerful affirmation of personal worth to enter the heart of the patient. Connecting them with the Divine at the end stage of this condition borders on the miraculous.

Affirmations of personal worth

Already presented throughout this chapter are the affirmations of personal worth. Personal worth belongs to every human being. One's theology about the worth of the human soul will come into clear focus in your practice of ministry to those with dementia. Every human being, regardless of the stage of their lives, merits dignity and respect. My hospice career reveals these two virtues daily. Every hospice clinician sees patients at their worst and most vulnerable moments. Ours is to give the highest and best care possible to these souls. Affirming their worth is vital to accomplishing this noble task. When we receive a patient with dementia, we know that their life's journey has been challenging. In the early and mid-stages of dementia, forgetfulness and odd behavior have played out in many scenarios. Perhaps a patient has taken a walk down the street from his or her home, frightening family who believed he or she was lost. Unfortunately, even the very best and most patient of caregivers have lost their patience and scolded loved ones or expressed disappointment in them. Being in the presence of many family caregivers reminds me that they need support. They need a place to vent, to release the inner pain and sorrow that dementia brings to a family. It can be said with confidence that when a family member gets sick with dementia, the entire family becomes sick.

Herein is why I urge faith communities to unite and walk with their congregants living with this condition. The caregiver is exhausted from long, sleepless nights and grueling days of caregiving. These long nights and challenging days begin to multiply, and the caregivers are in desperate need of care.

During these "bad" days, as caregivers say, the person with dementia hears negative, cutting statements that assail his or her self-worth. As these self-worth slayers mount, the person begins to withdraw. Only the person knows the depth of hurt and pain he or she feels. We can project from our own sense of experience how they might feel. Therefore, if we are going to offer patients spiritual support, affirmations of personal worth are necessary. Any religious system offers emotional support to its adherents. By transfer of thought to the patient, we can bless each with a sense of self-worth. Beyond that, we learn from patients who are not at end stage what their lives are like. I still hear echoing in my mind statements such as, "Chaplain Rich, I am losing my mind," "Chaplain Rich, I am having night terrors," "Chaplain Rich, I feel like I'm sinking like a ship." Losing one's mind and knowing it is frightening. Experiencing night terrors, waking up in the middle of the night with one's heart pounding and eyes wide open as if seeing a horrible image, is unimaginable. Sinking like a ship provides imagery that causes us deep sorrow for the patient.

Until the patient dies, they need affirmations of their personal worth. By the end stage of this pernicious condition, only a few words at a time can be processed. The affirmations must be short and potent. Here is a list of the most common affirmations:

- *You matter.* Affirming the fact that the patient's life still has meaning is vital.

- *You matter to God.* If life has meaning, then their soul has infinite worth. They may have forgotten God, but God has not forgotten them.

- *You matter to me.* Always state this with conviction and sincerity.

- *You are special.* Having spoken to over a thousand family caregivers, one thing I know is that the patient holds a place in the hearts of the family member that cannot be replaced. The patient is special, indeed.

- *You are special to God.* Relationships are everything at the end stage of any condition. It is no different with dementia. In time, this soul will take its journey home. They need to know that God sees them as special.

- *God loves you.* Though a theological concept, the soul needs to know love from God. I have seen ministers and missionaries long for that love. This affirmation allays fear of alienation from God.

- *You are a child of God.* During an awakening, the patient can receive this simple message. We help them connect with the God who considers them His own.

- *You are safe.* Night terrors, experiences in a nursing facility (no matter how posh and caring), loss of strength and awareness all reveal the need for safety. "You are safe" is one of the most important messages a spiritual caregiver can relate. I would like to think that for the moment in which it is spoken the patient does feel safe and secure. How awful to feel unsafe and insecure day after day? What relief it is to hear the words "You are safe."

The spiritual caregiver, during an awakening, practices a ministry of affirmation with these powerful words. Words do have power. It was words sung that triggered a memory or it was words related to a photo that triggered a memory, and it will be words spoken during the awakening that will find their way to the soul. Is this any different to what is hoped for in a faith community when the sacred is sung or read or spoken? Of course it isn't. These powerful words appear like beacons to a person living with dementia. They appear as a neon sign becoming the message to the soul that God still cares.

Vincent van Gogh's painting "The Church at Auvers" reminds me of the absence of spiritual care for the patient with end-stage dementia. The reader may research this masterpiece for a better view than my words can depict. This painting held deep meaning for van Gogh, but I see in this masterpiece significant meaning for the person with dementia as there is a striking similarity of messaging. There are paths that take one toward the church and around the church, but there is none to the church. Further, if there were a path to the church, surely there would be a path that leads one to the door of the church. Alas, there is no door to the church. It simply is not there. Indeed, how like the person with dementia is this painting. The soul is no longer aware that there is a path to God because that path is forgotten. A thick and ever-thickening fog has fallen on the mind of the patient. If the patient could speak, she might cry out, "God? Who? Church? What?" Yes, the patient with dementia finds life challenging and stressful. That is until you, the spiritual caregiver, come forth with a lantern of light with your photographs, your songs, your spritzers with aromas, your affirmations, and, now, your symbols and tactile objects.

Tactile objects

Adding to the senses already stimulated is the tactile experience. Roman Catholic patients respond well to having the rosary placed in their hands. It is very unfortunate when a patient enters the end stage of dementia that the deeply held religious traditions are neglected and no longer practiced for the patient. The rosary brings great comfort to Roman Catholic adherents. There is no more important time in the life of the patient than when he is in the land of forgetfulness to know that God still cares for him. In my experience, when placing the rosary in the hand of the patient, it helps to say the rosary with the patient. I am not of the Catholic faith, but because I am a chaplain, I have the rosary in my toolkit of religious rituals. By the time you use the rosary, you have shown the patient a series of photographs, spritzed the air with an aroma, and sung several songs. It does take time and effort to elicit an awakening. Never grow impatient; instead, lovingly take your time.

The sense of touch triggers the memory of the patient in a profound manner. One of the tactiles we use is the military patch. For those who may have a concern about post-traumatic stress disorder, we are sensitive to that and do our homework about the patient and his or her military service. I have seen patients hold the patch, rub the patch, kiss the patch, and salute the patch. It is an amazing sight to behold. Military service and all that is involved never leaves a veteran. This is true across the board and also relates to military veterans from other countries. The entire Dementia Care Protocol crosses ethnic, language, and religious barriers. If you are reading this book in Europe or the Middle East, or anywhere else for that matter, each piece of the Dementia Care Protocol is adaptable.

Those whose religious faith is Roman Catholic are drawn to the rosary. It brings comfort and triggers positive memories. Watching the person with dementia hold the beads as if he or she were saying the rosary is particularly gratifying. If you are a Catholic volunteer learning to use the Dementia Care Protocol, your church more than likely has a number of plastic rosary sets for use in hospitals or nursing facilities. The plastic rosary is preferred over the more expensive rosary due to the fact that in a nursing facility the rosary may be "borrowed" by another resident. As the patient holds the beads, it is very helpful to recite the rosary for the patient. There are instances when the patient will mouth the words or say a few words related to the rosary. Never despair should the patient ignore or not respond to the military patch or the rosary. It is the nature of the disease process. Be consistent and persistent, and the awakening will occur.

Symbols

The symbols are simple: models of a church, a temple, or a mosque; and a copy of sacred texts from the religious tradition of the patient. These symbols are used in the worship experience for the persons with dementia.

Worship program

If you are the imam and there are several patients in the memory care unit where you are doing your Dementia Care Protocol, gather them at a day and time which is convenient for them. The mornings are usually the best time of day for most persons with dementia. They have awakened from sleep, eaten, bathed, and dressed. The imam would ask for assistance from the facility staff to gather the Muslim patients together for worship. For all religious systems, the elements of the program are the same. Simplicity is the key to a public worship experience.

- *Call to worship.* Place the model of the mosque on a table so the patients can see it. Hold it up for them as you present the sacred reading and prayer. Both the sacred reading and prayer are brief and very familiar passages and prayers.

- *Singing.* Select songs the patients know from their past. I urge vocals only. The harmonies tend to make following the words of the song nearly impossible.

- *Individual worship time.* The assumption is that the imam has trained several volunteers who would come to the worship experience and use the specialty photos, music, aroma, affirmations of personal worth, and tactile objects. That the volunteers are present with the patients individually allows the patient to experience spirituality rather than just drop off to sleep. When the volunteers have completed their work with the patients, the imam may say a blessing and conclude the program.

The three facets of the worship experience allow for the patient to receive individualized guidance from the trained volunteers. If you are a priest, pastor, rabbi, or other religious leader/director, simply insert your role into the above directive for worship. The worship experience for a patient at the end stage of dementia is far different to for patients with other maladies and requires several volunteers to assist.

This scenario reveals the necessity of gentle persistence. As you will read, the patient did not respond to my first approach. I tried another. That is the nature of the multisensory intervention. What I have designed gives you options and if one thing doesn't seem to cause an awakening, perhaps another intervention will. You will see this as you read through this pastoral care encounter.

Scenario One

The patient presented as an 83-year-old female, who was in her bed in the facility. Her religious background was Roman Catholic. Her family indicated she liked "Amazing Grace," "In the Garden," and "Ave Maria." I used the photograph series "In the Garden," showing her several roses while singing "In the Garden." The spritz added to the experience. There was no indication of an awakening at that point, so I changed gears and sang "Ave Maria" (not an easy song to sing, but keep in mind that any challenge to me is mine to embrace as the patient's needs are greater than my need for comfort). The patient opened her eyes and looked at me. This was a clear indication of an awakening. I then placed the rosary in her hands and recited the rosary. A tear welled up in her eye and coursed down her cheek. I shared several affirmations: "God loves you," "God cares for you," "You matter to God," "You are safe," "God is here." Her body noticeably relaxed.

The question might arise as to the tempo of my speech when speaking the affirmations. My body language was relaxed and open as I spoke the affirmations. I looked at her eyes with a gentle look. I spoke the affirmations slowly with compassion. This is how it is done. One of the greatest examples for me of compassionate ministry is Jesus Christ. When reading about how he spoke to the sick and dying or even the dead, he did so with a gentleness and compassion that serves as a constant reminder to me of how to practice effective pastoral care.

In this pastoral care encounter, you will see that I was prepared with several different pieces of the multisensory intervention. It is always best to have several options at hand. Further, you will read that when the awakening occurred, I stopped using any further interventions and instead, used the affirmations of personal worth. The window of opportunity is usually open briefly; therefore, I provided the affirmations while the window of opportunity was open.

Scenario Two

The patient presented as an 85-year-old male who was in his wheelchair in the common area of the facility. I felt it best to conduct the visit there. Only two patients were there, and they were sleeping. I focused on his military service as the family indicated his military career was something he cherished. They also mentioned that his faith in God was very important to him. He served his church in many volunteer capacities. In his room, I noticed from previous visits he has several photos of his military experience and hats with military emblems emblazoned on them. I did not jump right in with the "Patriot Series" of photos but used the "Snack Time" photos. He loved chocolate chip cookies, so I spritzed the chocolate chip cookie aroma and showed him the photographs of chocolate chip cookies and other snacks. He showed interest in what I was doing. I then transitioned to using the "Patriot Series" of photographs and showed the American flag and sang the National Anthem. He put his hands on the armrests of the wheelchair and appeared as if he were trying to stand. Obviously, we were in the midst of an awakening. Upon completion of the singing, I thanked him for his service to the country and related, "You are special," "You are special to God," "God loves you," "God cares for you." This experience taught me that although I planned to place the patch of his branch of the military in his hands, an awakening had occurred. There would be another time when I would use this.

In each of the above scenarios, I stayed with the patient for the sake of pastoral presence. Being with the patient humming tunes or reading brief sacred writings fills the visit with spirituality. Spirituality is often a missing virtue at the end stage of dementia and one that finds its place in the heart of the patient when using the multisensory intervention.

I firmly believe that the religious institutions of all countries need to embrace the Dementia Care Protocol to provide a loving, supportive experience for their countrymen and women who are living with dementia in all its forms. These persons can respond and need the inner inspiration that worship can bring. As I have written several times, they may have forgotten God, but God has not forgotten them. Bringing the message of the sacred is, indeed, your privilege.

In training meetings, there have been questions about the use of the various parts of the Dementia Care Protocol. Chaplains have asked if they have to use all the parts of it to be successful. No, one does not have to use all the parts of the Protocol to be successful. In fact, there will be circumstances when that is simply not possible. A person with dementia might not be able to see due to the condition or for some other reason. So don't use the photographs; instead, use singing, affirmations of personal worth, and/or tactile objects. As you gain experience in the use of the multisensory intervention, you will develop a sense of what will or won't work in that encounter. Keep in mind that you are doing what others are not doing mainly because others do not know what can be done. You will carry with you a toolkit that others aren't aware of. Whatever pieces you use will go a long way toward caring for the person with dementia. In the final analysis, use what you can and pray that your patient receives comfort and peace through your efforts.

Conclusion

The world is full of talk. What we need is action.[1]

The purpose of the conclusion of a book of this nature is to review the salient points I have tried to make and put them in motion. There are several bedrock matters that require recall. The first is the philosophy of the Dementia Care Protocol. For the multisensory intervention to succeed, the spiritual caregiver must embrace this philosophy. The philosophy honors the personhood of all people living with dementia. There are those who describe people with dementia as living in a bubble with no substantive connection to the real world. Yes, they eat, sleep, but they toilet in adult diapers, and must be bathed and clothed by others. They only exist and wait to die. What a harsh statement: they exist and wait to die.

What I have placed in your hands is a means to ensure that these souls do more than exist until they die. Their condition is disabling. Their condition takes them to a challenging and stressful place. However, since we know where their residence is, we can use the multisensory intervention to find them. It is hoped that my words of encouragement and admonition will stir professional chaplains to learn and implement the intervention.

---

1   Author's own words.

It is also hoped that those leading faith communities will act on the Dementia Care Protocol. I will continue to advocate for ministry to the dementia patient and his or her caregiver. There are tens of thousands of patients and caregivers in any region of any state and nation who would welcome a loving faith community to come along beside them in their journey through dementia. Will this book incite an awakening of this need? Time will tell.

Further, there are tens of thousands of people with dementia in nursing facilities and more in their own homes being cared for by family. Some of these are in hospice care; others are not. Regardless, chaplains and spiritual caregivers need to embrace a means to provide effective spiritual support for these patients. It is not enough to enter a patient's room, observe the depth to which the condition has taken the patient, and only offer a prayer and depart. That is sub-par spiritual care. As I related my story of the early days of my chaplaincy, I knew there had to be more I could do to provide spiritual care. I recognized the charge I was given to provide spiritual support, so I had to find a way to accomplish this task. The Dementia Care Protocol is the means to fulfill this charge.

Regarding the photographs you will view on the publisher's website, they are unique in that they capture one thing only and have a minimum of background clutter. Are these the only photographs that can be used? Absolutely not! I am constantly in search of new photographs that will communicate with the patient. I urge you to do likewise. This is not a completed study, but an ongoing endeavor to meet the needs of patients. Join me in this effort. Share your discoveries. Dementia in all its forms is not cureable at this time and will only increase in its spread across the globe. Therefore, all of you committed to making a difference in the lives of patients will explore new means to provide effective spiritual support.

In talking with one of my chaplain team members, he shared that the Dementia Care Protocol has changed the direction of his chaplaincy career. He has given his life to exploring how to communicate with dementia patients. He is an expert in the Dementia Care Protocol. Cornerstone Hospice & Palliative Care is the epicenter of a movement to support persons with dementia in this unique multisensory intervention.

Lastly, I want you to know that the multisensory intervention crosses all barriers. It is adaptable to all religious systems as you, the professional spiritual care practitioner, can come up with appropriate photographs and songs that apply specifically to your faith community. The caveat that I offer is that the photographs need to have minimal background clutter and the image needs to be brilliant in color. The songs you select need to be sung rather than played on a device. The person with dementia cannot distinguish the melody when harmonies are present. Use your voice. Do not allow personal awkwardness to prevent you from using your voice. Add to the affirmations of personal worth. Keep them brief and clear. I recall the experience in sharing songs with a patient who appeared to be non-responsive. I sang several songs he was familiar with and shared a few affirmations, one being "God loves you." His back was toward me the entire visit, so I did not think I had communicated until the patient replied, "Really?" You will never know the extent of your impact on a patient.

To all reading this work, jettison the myth that you must have results. This Western cultural standard is a creativity killer in providing spiritual support. Be creative. Think of additional symbols and ways to provide worship. I caution you not to adopt a traditional "order of worship" for your worship services. That won't work. You must take your team of trained Dementia Care Protocol workers with you to provide individualized worship experiences for those in attendance. Dream big and make the dream come to pass in your ministry.

The second focus must be on the caregivers. I have spoken to many groups of caregivers. There is a common theme: exhaustion. What a great blessing it would be for your organization—be it a hospice or faith community—to have a quarterly or otherwise regular meeting for the caregivers and have a lighthearted program so they can unwind and enjoy themselves for an hour or two. Provide a support group for these angels of mercy. They will be blessed and, in turn, bless you.

So, as we close this guide to dementia care, may you experience the joy of serving well the population of people with dementia on your caseload as a professional chaplain or spiritual caregiver, or those who live in the area of influence of your faith community. Please let me know how your ministry is going.

References

Alzheimer's Association (2017) "Quick Facts." Accessed on 19/02/2018 at www.alz.org/facts.

Davis, R. (1989) *My Journey into Alzheimer's Disease*. Carol Stream, IL: Tyndale House Publishers.

Gardiner, L. (2012) Quotation from Dementia Positive website. From a conference speech in September 2012. Accessed on 19/02/2018 at www.dementiapositive.co.uk/previous-quotations-of-the-month.html.

Greenblat, C. (2012) *Love, Loss, and Laughter: Seeing Alzheimer's Differently*. Guilford, CT: Lyons Press.

Leggett, A.N., Zarit, S., Taylor, A. and Galvin, J.E. (2011) "Stress and burden among caregivers of patients with Lewy body dementia." *The Gerontologist 51*, 1, 76–85. Accessed on 19/02/2018 at https://academic.oup.com/gerontologist/article/51/1/76/627002.

Mayo Clinic (2018) "Lewy body dementia." Accessed on 19/02/2018 at www.mayoclinic.org/diseases-conditions/lewy-body-dementia/symptoms/causes/syc-20352025.

Mo (2007) "Alois Alzheimer's First Case." *ScienceBlogs*. Accessed on 19/02/2018 at http://scienceblogs.com/neurophilosophy/2007/11/02/alois-alzheimers-first-case.

Reisberg, B. (1988) "Functional Assessment Staging (FAST)." *Psychopharmocology Bulletin 24*, 653–659.

Shamy, E. (2003) *A Guide to the Spiritual Dimension of Care for People with Alzheimer's Disease and Related Dementia: More than Body, Brain and Breath*. London: Jessica Kingsley Publishers.

Tomlinson, B.E., Blessed, G. and Roth, M. (1970) "Observations on the brains of demented old people." *Journal of the Neurological Sciences 11*, 3, 205–242. Accessed on 19/02/2018 at www.jns-journal.com/article/0022-510X(70)90063-8/pdf.

Tang-Wai, D.F. and Graham, N.L. (2008) "Assessment of language function in dementia." *Geriatrics and Aging 11*, 2, 103–110.

Zeisal, J. (2009) *I'm Still Here: A New Philosophy of Alzheimer's Care.* New York: Penguin Group.

Afterword

It is with great honor that I share with you the exciting process that began for me over six years ago. Serving as a chaplain in an assisted-living facility that cares for persons with dementia, I spent many hours listening and talking to the residents concerning their lives.

It was also at the same time that I was working on my Master's Degree in Ministry where all my electives were in psychology, especially those dealing with dementia. I believed God put me at this facility to care for these persons stricken with dementia. Dr. Rich Behers, who was working in hospice came into my life through our church relationship. We connected because of our common interest in ministry to those with dementia. He discovered as did I that those with dementia cannot pick out specific items in a magazine photograph or other type of photograph that has multiple items in it. He discovered that the person with dementia could best recognize the contents of a photograph of one thing only. We agreed to work together on a project making a catalogue of specialty photographs. He gave me a subject list of photographs he needed, and we started working on them. It has been amazing how God brought us together to work on this project. The results have truly been a blessing not only to them but to us. I used these photographs at the long-term care facility I served, and Dr. Rich used them in his hospice work. He expanded this project into the Dementia Care Protocol which added aromas, music, and affirmations of personal worth.

The photographs are simple and have only one focal point, such as a single flower, a flag, a bird, an animal, or a cookie, just to name a few. One thing I learned quickly was that persons with dementia wanted to see the same images over and over again. It is something they can relate to and it is somewhat familiar when they see it again. I could never have imagined when I snapped those pictures that it would help so many people to such an extent. As I reflect on the photographs and all that has been done with them, I cherish the stories they have brought about and I give praises to the God who brought it all about.

Carol Gilmore
photographer and educator

Index